# Con

Introduction

1. All Saints - the Early Years
   *by John Rushton & Raymond Hayes*

2. Rebuild and Redesign

3. The Bells of All Saints

4. Kirkbymoorside's Choral Interest

5. All Saints' Church House

6. Churchyard and the Memorials

7. The Vicars and the Vicarage

8. Sunday School and the Junior Church

9. The Church of Today

10. The Petch Family of KMS
    *by Jean Richards*

11. Extracts from the Parish Magazine 1919 - 1939

## Introduction

Seated at the top of the town of Kirkbymoorside, All Saints Church has witnessed much over its lifetime and has undergone many changes to its appearance. However one thing remains unchanged, that of its importance to the community.

The importance of Ryedale to the early Christian movements is clear from the number of monasteries and churches whose origins date back to the 700s. St Mary's Church at Lastingham and the connection to St Chad and St Cedd all show the spread of Christianity from Northumberland and Whitby down through rural Yorkshire. Its remoteness and tranquility were the ideal conditions for spiritual contemplation and discovery. However the area also attracted Scandinavian raiders keen to loot any treasures and goods from this fertile farming area. As a result many original stone and wooden structures suffered and were pulled down or destroyed.

However, once the raiders became settlers the early churches were rebuilt in stone. The area has many wonderful churches hidden in the villages around Ryedale.

St Gregory's is one of the best known gems. Situated within a couple of miles from All Saints Church, this is one of the smallest known minsters, along with nearby Stonegrave. A minster denotes an ecclesiastic centre - some are very

grand and were seats of power very much like the great cathedrals of Durham and Winchester. Others acted as mother churches with a small community of monks and nuns along with lay people who would minister to outlying villages. Both Kirkdale and Stonegrave fall into this category.

Within Kirkbymoorside today there are three other remaining active churches.

St Chad's Catholic Church in Piercy End was opened in 1897, shown above before the encroachment of houses, following the abandonment of an earlier chapel in Tinley Garth. A full history of St Chad's has been compiled by Lucy Warrack.

Hidden at the bottom of West End is the Friend's Meeting House. Established in 1691, the Quaker community remains as active and as welcoming as ever.

Several Methodist Chapels have been lost as places of worship. However the Methodist Chapel in Piercy End celebrates its bi-centenary this year (2012) and the attached room is well used by the local community for meetings and clubs such as Rainbows and Brownies.

# Chapter One: History of the Parish *written by John Rushton and R H Hayes*

Kirkby and its Church survived the coming of the Normans relatively unscathed. The men at the Hall, the ten farmers and the miller at Kirkby Mills on the river Dove were still actively producing their crops in 1086 from the arable land of the lower hill slopes, although many local villages were denuded of population. Probably, the church was already sustained by the tithes of the farmer's produce, the tenth of any increase in crops which early farmers devoted to the work of charity and the spirit. The first Norman lord of Kirkby—Sherif Hugh Fitzbaldric, gave some of his outlying estates to the revived monastery of Whitby, whose persecuted monks moved to found the Abbey of St. Mary's, York. His successor, the first Robert de Stuteville, added the tithes of his Kirkby demesnes to St. Mary's endowment, but he, and the Earl of Mortain, overlord of Fadmoor, lost their estates to the Crown as a result of rebellion and the gift was revoked. King Henry offered the Church, with others at Coxwold and Hovingham to Bishop Robert of Lincoln, but again this gift was not permanent.

The Kirkby estates were regranted to Nigel d' Albini, father of the Mowbray family and his son Roger offered the Church to the Abbot of the new Cistercian monastery he had founded at Byland. The Abbot refused, on the grounds that Roger de Mowbray had already done enough for them, but the baron is said to have taken great offence at the refusal. Soon afterwards he made Kirkby Moorside Church and its incomes part of the endowment of his new foundation, the Augustinian Priory of Newburgh, adding to the gift, one fifth of the Kirkby field land—a carucate—and the houses associated with it, which had probably long formed the estate of the church, as well as his church at Welburn. Henceforth canons of Newburgh Priory served as priests in the Churches, while the Priory maintained the chancel and received the revenues.

In mediaeval records of 1154-69, William the clerk of Kirkby often appears, together with his colleague Ingelram, Dean of Ryedale and presbyter of Welburn. During this period, the stone church was rebuilt, and c 1183-99, a chaplain called Hugh was appointed to reside at Gillamoor Chapel. William de Stuteville agreed with Prior Bernard that Hugh and his successors at Gillamoor should sing daily masses for the souls of William and his parents, and shortly afterwards he endowed the chapel with field lands and pasture rights on the commons above the village.

The third Robert de Stuteville had recovered his grandfather's estates by 1183, but by that time the Mowbrays had already given parts of the property to the monasteries whose influence was rapidly extending through the district. Rievaulx Abbey had gained the clearing at Middlehead in Farndale where Edmund the Hernit had lived, as well as Dowthwaite and pasture in Farndale. St. Mary's Abbey had developed an important grange at Spaunton whose men took their beasts to pasture there. Now Stuteville and his son endowed their own monastic house within the bounds of Kirkby Moorside. Robert settled a community of nuns at Keldholme, where the site of their inclosure and garden is still easily discovered, even though their buildings have gone. At Keldholme the Prioress,

Above: Ernest Collier worked as the sextant so was responsible for digging graves, cutting grass and maintaining the boilers. He found the silver coin (right) in 1965.

Shown here are some of the pieces of original stonework removed in 1875 from All Saints and now housed at the Ryedale Folk Museum, Hutton-le-Hole since 1970.

Right: St Mary's Farndale

Below: St Aidan's Gillamoor

Above: St Michael's Gt Edstone

Left: St Nicholas' Bransdale

the nuns, and their lay brothers and servants built a Church of the Blessed Mary, with a cloister, chapter-house, refectory, dormitory and hall. In the outer precinct were the farm buildings, from which they managed their arable, meadow and pasture lands, around the house, at Ravenswick, Farndale and Bransdale. From the woods of Ravenswick came the bark for their tannery. A priest named Master Geoffrey of Dove supervised the distant properties which other donors had given them at Ingleby, Rook Barugh, Edstone, Cropton and Habton.

By this time, the Stuteville's may have established their castle, the well-defined moat of which can still be seen in the Applegarth Field behind the Church, and behind which was their large deer park. Under Nicholas and Joan de Stuteville, and her husband and son, Hugh le Bigod and Baldwin Wake, the castle brought fresh stimulus to the town and its church. Sheepfolds were built on the moors. Five water mills sprang up on the dale streams, and a common oven served the bakers of the town. More than 150 families settled in Farndale and Bransdale and to serve the growing populace of the district a weekly market was begun, with a fair on the patronal feast day of Keldholme Priory, the Eve, Day and Morrow of the Nativity of Mary. Every year, the townsmen took in dues to the Manor Lord, their Christmas hens, and at harvest time, they moved the tithe crops to the great barn of the Church.

Kirkby Moorside Church was expanded, its chancel modified, side aisles added to its nave, to meet the growing demand. The ageing Vicar Geoffrey had presbyter William of Tunstall in 1281, and Walter, Rector of Gilling in 1283, appointed to assist him as co-adjutors. Three years later, when the old man was quite blind, Thomas the rector of Barton in Ryedale succeeded them as his guardian. Then, in 1288, the Archdeacon of Cleveland came to induct Sir William de Hextildesham, the chaplain presented as his successor by the Prior and Convent of Newburgh, but towards the close of the century the Prior was charged by Archbishop Greenfield with failing to appoint perpetual vicars. One such a vicar was appointed, he enjoyed a definite share of the tithes. Certainly the Vicar already had one definite income, a payment in money of 13/4 a year, in place of the tithes of Kirkby Mill. Together with the Prioress's right in the mill, valued at 26/8, his dues there had been commuted for a fixed money payment before 1276. Taken together the two payments formed one tenth of the mill's annual value.

With its carucate of land, and extensive tithe rights, the Church was closely involved in day to day farming life. In 1276, ten of the town's cottagers held their tenements and lands from the Church, but the parson may well have worked his own land. Similarly the Keldholme Prioress cultivated wide lands, and from her farm at Moorhouses managed the sheep flocks, whose sacks of wool sold to Italian merchants, paid for leading the Convent roof and embellishing its buildings. Despite its wealth, the Priory entered a period of difficulty in the early 14th century, when rising living standards, mismanagement and the waywardness of some aristocratic nuns involved the Kirkby Vicars in attempts to reform the convent.

Severe penances were imposed on recalcitrants, and nuns were ordered to cease bringing their puppies into the choir, and to render obedience to the Prioress. When the townsmen interfered in the election of a Prioress, Nicholas de Rephingale, a prominent townsman, was excommunicated, and later required to do penances at York Minster, and at Kirkby and Keldholme churches. The Kirkby Vicar and the Ryedale dean were called in to supervise the elections.

By this time, another church building had been built in the parish—the Chapel of the Brethren of the Trinity in Farndale. Little is known of the life of the Brothers but for perhaps 150 years, the manor lords of Kirkby appointed their priest. Some associate them with the old inn on the Blakey ridgeway. Possibly the first chapel at Cocken in Bransdale also came into existence, in these years before the pestilence checked the growth of population and reduced the amount of cultivated land. When the Wake family left the town, and distant landlords allowed the castle to decay, Kirkby's taxes were reduced, men of Farndale and Bransdale broke into the Prioress's Moorhouse and stole her goods, and there were ominous reports of raids on the deerpark and riots in the market place. The legend that the Neville family rebuilt the Church after houses between the Church and Stuteville Castle had been burnt down, may yet be found to have some foundation in fact.

The Nevilles, a prominent northern family, came to the town early in the 15th century. They were probably responsible for building the town's second "castle" or fortified manor house, which gave its name to "Castlegate", and led the town to grow northwards towards Manor Vale. In the Church, the family saw the 15th century timber roof installed, with its elaborate moulded ridges, principals and purlins. At the intersections, some of the bosses still carry the Neville coat of arms. In the same century, the south porch and the west tower were built, and the easternmost aisle columns and the chancel arch were reconstructed. The porch was given a small parvise chamber over its barrelled entry, with a low pitched roof and embattled parapets. The room can be reached from the stone steps inside the Church. According to tradition, it accommodated monks from Newburgh Priory staying overnight, and was later used as a store for muniments.

The mass dial on the outside of the porch was to lose its old function a hundred years later, as the religious climate began to change, but in 1527, one of the Kirkby chaplains could still leave his body to be buried in the church or churchyard of All Hallowes at Kirkby Moorside, and his soul to "Almight God", to the "Glorious Mother Mary" and the "Holy Company in Heaven", with money provided for "a hoole trentall" to be celebrated on the day of his burial, and with pennies for distribution at "dirige and messe" that day, 2d to every parish clerk, and a 1d for every scholar. He willed his velvet hood to the church to make a corporal.

As the social and political changes leading to the English "reformation" gathered strength, there were hints of change at Kirkby. Nicholas Sonley, a priest at Welburn confessed that he had married

Isabella Chapley, but was ordered no longer to consort with her. The priest of "Coken Kirke" in Bransdale was accused of treasonable words spoken in his chapel to the parish clerk, by William Wood of Kirkby. In response the chaplain threatened "to have, of him, either a leg, or an arm, if he informed against him". The churchwardens and sworn men complained in 1567, that Henry Dail, clerk of Coken and Kirkby "dothe not celebrate or read the devine service plainlie and distinctlie that the hearers may be edified", but rather did "but mumble uppe the same". After trial at York Cathedral, his licence to preach was withdrawn.

Newburgh Priory in its last years let off the Rectory and its greater tithes to laymen for a fixed rent. The lessee collected what tithes he could, and being more pertinaceous in his efforts, encountered more resistance. Laurence Lepton, the lessee in 1546 had trouble securing the tithe of trees felled by Urpinus Gilpin. The Vicar too had similar trouble. After the Priory was dissolved, the diversion of the tithe revenues to laymen resulted in neglect of the church. The wardens in 1575 reported that the chancel had been in great ruin and decay for seven years past, both in walls, glass windows and leads, and said that they thought Robert Constable, farmer of the "parsonage" ought to repair it.

The old Priory at Keldholme was also swept away to provide revenues for the Crown. The Prioress was given a pension, the nuns scattered, some to marry, and the Earl of Westmoreland, a Neville, was given the site, its lands and rentals. Sir John Potter, the last chaplain shortly before the dissolution had a life grant of the chaplain's house at Keldholme. Within a few years the Priory buildings were to decay, although the last fragments were not cleared away till the early 19th century. Twenty pounds worth of lead from the Church roof, and two bells were sold immediately but the stone long provided a handy quarry. The jewels, worth 74/6, and the farmstock were closely accounted for, but no more was ever heard of the relics—the "piece of the True Cross" and the "finger of St. Stephen" which had once been lent to lying in women. Today, only a burial slab or two, a few stones and some earthworks survive from the Priory.

The Catholic Nevilles of Kirkby were involved in the Yorkshire revolt of 1569, when men were reported to be gathering in a rebellious manner at the town. Charles Neville, Earl of Westmoreland, is traditionally reported to have escaped to Scotland over snow-covered ground to the north, by reversing the shoes of his horse to mislead pursuers. The descendants of the blacksmith who performed the work are said to have enjoyed their Castlegate house at a ¼d a year rent for long times afterwards. In the 19th century a burial stone, described as being under the chancel, was said to carry the blacksmith's arms on its reverse side in commemoration of the event.

Another prominent family who left a distinctive memorial in the Church were the Brooke's relatives of the Nevilles. They seem to have bought old monastic property at Kirkdale, including the old Rievaulx Abbey Grange at Sonley Cote, during Henry the Eighth's

Stone faces look out over the hills from the altar window

reign. When Lady Brooke died during July 1600, the monument to record her passing was inscribed with a portrayal of her six sons and five daughters, kneeling around her in the costume of the time. The brass plate can be seen near the altar rail mounted in a frame of Derbyshire marble, with panels of black marble inset carrying inscriptions. One tells that she was "a good woman, a very good mother, and an exceedingly good wife". The other advises that "Her soule is at rest with God, for she was sure that her redeemer lived, and that though worms destroyed her body, yet she should see God in the flesh".

"Reader, Prepare for Death, for if the fatall sheares,
Could have bene stay'd, by prayers, sighes, or teares,
They had bene stay'd, and this tomb thou see'st here,
Had not erected beene, yet many a yeare."

The plaque covered a grave in the church floor, but its slab was taken up and long used to block one of the old south windows.

As long-established religious opinions changed, and matters of faith became closely connected with political loyalties, the long struggle for religious freedom began. Both Catholics and Puritans saw periods of persecution. One family at Gillamoor and several more at Kirkdale kept their Catholic faith well into the 17th century, but the situation was such that in 1611, a Wellburn villager could report that he had seen ten or more people carrying Catholic widow Pearson's body to a midnight secret burial in Kirkdale churchyard. By 1651, another wing of religious faith was organised at Kirkby Moorside, the Society of Friends, and in the early years of the next century a Quaker burial ground was formed in Farndale. It may be that Kirkby Church was the one that George Fox refused to go into in 1651, because it was so much painted.

The established Church continued its work, although shorn of some of its revenues; but for a brief space, during the "Puritan Revolution" there were extreme changes. William Lack was "minister" at Kirkby then, and "solemnisation of marriage" ceremonies were carried out in the presence of the Puritan Justice of the Peace, Luke Robinson. One William Sturdy was appointed "parish register" but the new system was shortlived. At the Restoration of the monarchy in 1660, Thomas Hardwick was appointed vicar, while in the next few years, the town's grammar school was revived, in the small room abutting the churchyard, whilst Cocken Chapel, sometimes called Thackwaite was given burial rights, and the Bransdale parishioners ceased to make the long trek to the mother church bearing coffins on their shoulders.

During the 17th century, the old Rectory house of "parsonage" enjoyed some prominence in the hands of laymen holding the rectory incomes on lease. It stood on the opposite side of the Market Place from the Church, and is there yet, although now known as the "Buckingham House" after its best-known visitor. The house was then the second largest in the town, abutting tithe barn lane to the south, the tithe barn being on the south side of this road, and the parsonage kiln, probably a malt kiln, to the north, where outbuildings of the King's Head Hotel now stand. Here lived the

Right: Stained Glass window in the vestry

Above and right: The memorial plaque dedicated to Lady Brooke showing her and her children kneeling in prayer

Nandyke family, one of whose number was the last Prioress of Wykeham, a lady who distributed alms to every house in Kirkby on the day she died. In 1614 they transferred the house to Vicar William Denton, who took several tenants to court for non-payment of tithes, and was himself charged with breaking into Francis Sleightholme's close to take timber, possibly in an attempt to assert his rights.

After Vicar Denton, Tobias Thurscrosse and Robert Otterbourne jointly held the rectory, and found themselves charged at Quarter Sessions in 1652-3 with neglecting repairs to the chancel. Younger sons of the Thurscrosse family acted as vicars, but Tobias himself was a Royalist landowner, heavily fined for his part in the Civil Wars, an event which may account for the neglect. In 1702 at Gillamoor and Fadmoor, and twelve years later at Kirkby, the Duncombe family, forbears of the Earls of Feversham, purchased the rectory, since when the churches have been better sustained. In 1687 a national figure died at the old parsonage house, his passing tersely recorded in the parish register—"1687, April 17th, Gorges Vilaus, Lord Dooke of Bockingham". The parson had prayers with him before he died. After embalming and laying in state, he was taken to Helmsley Castle and then to Westminster for burial.

At the Church, many of the internal furnishings had now been changed to suit the reformed modes of worship. The older masses had given way to preaching services based on the Authorised Version of the Bible and the Prayer Book. Communion became important, and a 17th century Jacobean table with fluted legs and an upper rail was installed. The old communion rails with twisted balusters can now be seen at Gillamoor Church, whence they were moved from Kirkby at a later date. A carved beam above the doorway at Gillamoor bearing the inscription "T.K;G.I:R.W;T.H. Churchwardens, H.S.I.1682." also memorialises the church officials who now acquired greater importance in parish affairs.

In the days of Tobias Thurscrosse, the Rectory incomes amounted to £50, and the vicar's revenues to £100, but by 1743, this sum was drawn by a Vicar who lived in London, Henry Maunder paid a curate £33.3.0 to serve his Parish Church and the dependant chapels, some 326 families in all, of whom two were Catholic and fifteen Quakers. The Society of Friends now had their own meeting house in the town, where about 40 people met once or twice a week. The curate Robert Mansell now lived in a vicarage on the south side of Tithe Barn Lane, where he had stables, but the tithe barn had been converted into a warehouse, and part of his plot let off as a blacksmith's shop.

At Kirkby Church, the Curate saw that his flock were baptised, confirmed, married and buried. There were morning and afternoon services, but one Sunday in three he rode out to Cockan and on the other two Sundays read a service at Gillamoor. In Lent he catechised the children of Kirkby and those who walked in from Gillamoor, visiting Cockan on August the 7th for the same purpose. Communions were still rare, five times a year at Kirkby and once a year at the two chapels. Of the 661 people qualified to come, 257

Carved faces around the exterior of the church

Above: Little Ryedale's gravestone

attended on Good Friday of that year. Occasionally, there was a public confession of immorality, and from time to time, there were more elaborate services when printed prayer sheets were brought from London. In 1746, a service was held "imploring assistance for our Arms, pardoning our sins, and for averting those heavy judgments which our manifold provocations have most justly deserved". Another in 1749 expressed thanks "for putting an end to the late bloody and expensive war".

The Reverend William Comber, a grandson of the famous divine, Dean Comber of Durham, exchanged his Lincolnshire living with that of the Kirkby Vicar in 1756, and came himself to live in the town. Men were to credit him with a great revival of church life, at a time when the town's population, industry and agriculture were once again expanding. For a time he also supervised Kirkdale Church. Comber "used every means in his power to suppress vice in the town" until his death in 1810. When he was taken to be buried in his family vault at Stonegrave Church, his "grateful hearers", who had worked with him for 54 years, erected a monument recording his "unceasing attention to their spiritual and temporal interests".

At first, Comber's revenues were still largely derived from tithes and from his glebe land. Many tithes came to him in kind, but from each of the mills he had small money payments instead. From every communicant, every house, and every yard at Kirkby he had 2d a year, and similar payments from the houses and garths of the outlying villages. A marriage brought him 2/6 to 10s, a funeral 1/6 to 2/6, and a churching 8d. His Gillamoor oxgang, and his Kirkby carucate of land, each divided into numerous strips in the fields, brought other moneys, and he let off his chapel yard and vicarage house at Gillamoor, and his meadow and Kirkbank at Cockan. Some of his land plots still bore ancient names like priest's tonque, priest's cap, Lady Land. While he was vicar, the open fields and commons were inclosed into small fields. After first opposing the Gillamoor inclosure of 1771-2, Comber gave way and was awarded two fields of nine acres in place of 27 smaller pieces. His Gillamoor rental rose from £3 to £6.10 and when Kirkby was inclosed, in 1788-93, there was a larger increase in his income.

Some of his revenues, Comber devoted to improving his Church. He brought curates to the town to help him, men like William Richardson, whose "good singing voice" and evangelical emphasis on "Justification by faith alone" led some to fear that he would become a Methodist, but which secured him a place as head of the vicars-choral of York Cathedral. While here he made great use of Thomas Robinson's theological library at Welburn, where a later Vicar of Kirkby, Edmund Gray, received his early instruction. In an age when Methodism was spreading its appeal through the dales, and finding a ready response, Kirkby Church was also pursuing an evangelical approach. Meanwhile, another denomination, the Congregationalists, had built a chapel at the town in 1793, and for some time afterwards sustained a minister in the town.

On New Year's Day, 1779, a tempestuous wind had blown a

The magnificent altar window

great sheet of lead weighing 300lb., from the top of the church, carrying it over the chancel, the churchyard and a house, until it landed in the street 60 yards away. By 1802, the church tower, for which Mrs Comber had given a clock seven years previously, was falling into ruins. Comber decided on a full scale reconstruction of the tower, and extensive repairs to the rest of the church. Above the ground stage, the tower was rebuilt, within a year, a parapet battlement and corner pinnacles replacing the older spire, and Mrs. Comber's clock was reinstalled on the south side. The old peal of three bells was removed and six new bells installed, a subscription being raised for the extra metal. The entire cost was £1,041, of which £219 was raised by sale of the scaffolding and the old bells. Three years later, as the remaining instalments were paid off, a small organ was bought at the expense of Mrs. Dorothy Comber and of George and Francis Atkinson, gentlemen and mercers who now occupied the old parsonage. Mrs. Comber and Ann Atkinson also left substantial sums for financing Christmas distributions to the poor. The Vicar endowed a book fund for the new Sunday School.

In that same year, 1802, Gillamoor Church was also reconstructed, almost in its entirety, although some of the old masonry and fittings were re-used. The small church, comprising a nave and chancel under one roof, still carries an unusual plaque as a memorial to the mason primarily responsible. "Here lie deposited the ashes of James Smith of Farndale, Stone Mason. He was a sound working man. And in consequence selected to rebuild this chapel, which he completed with his own hands in the summer of 1802. He died Oct. 31, 1819. Aged 64 years." In the burial yard, but a few feet away are the resting places of others of his generation, including John Clayton whose stone, erected in 1817, records that "He was a local preacher in the Methodist Connexion, 44 years". During the course of the Gillamoor reconstruction, the ancient Norman font was also placed in the church yard, and replaced by what a later writer was to call "an unsightly apology for a font".

Vicars Joseph Smyth and Edmund Gray continued the work with their parishioners which Comber had begun. The organ was improved in 1818, by a self-taught musician, Thomas Gray of Pickering, but the instrument was almost destroyed by fire in the following winter when a lighted candle fell into it. Not surprisingly we find the Churchwardens ordering two candlesticks shortly afterwards, and the township subscribing for Gray to build a larger instrument during the twenties. As hymn tunes were popularised, church music became more important. Bell-ringing became something more than the parish clerk's telling of the morning and evening bells, as change-ringers gathered to sound the peals for Coronations, Royal birthdays and festivals.

In this era, the Church was filled with "great high pews, up to the communion rails", to provide warmth and to exclude inclement winds from the sermon audiences. The rapid growth of Kirkby's population brought every available space into use, and inside the pews, stoves were installed, burning the coals brought in regular

Above and below: Original carved faces on the south side of the vestry

shipments from Malton to fuel them. A toilet was built in 1823, and equipped with its own lantern and snufflers. A new ceiling was built above the organ, and in 1824 a new gallery with 31 more pews. The next year George Potter installed a plaster ceiling right throughout the church, with chandeliers fixed beneath it on pulleys. A north gallery was added in 1827. As the coals gave off smoke, the parish clerk became more involved in cleaning the church than keeping its records, and three ladies were taken on annually to clean the pews. Mrs. Shepherd of Douthwaite endowed one pew to be made available for visitors staying at the White Horse Inn. Outside, the churchyard was improved as well—a notice posted forbidding games, flagged pathways made, and the old sundial fenced in. Even the bridge in the yard was improved, possibly to give an easier exit from the church tower for the town fire-engine.

Mr. Smyth and Mr. Gray were donors of much of the old parish plate. Joseph Smyth gave a communion cup of silver dated 1724, a chalice, paten and flagon. Edmund Gray presented a chalice with cover, and an old loving cup of 1712. As a result, the older silver chalice and salver were sold to the Churchwardens of Gillamoor. Interest in ceremonial was increasing, and crimson cloth and Irish linen appeared amongst the purchases of the churchwardens. By mid-century, another vestige of the past was swept away, when money payments were substituted for older tithe payments in kind. Until this time, the Vicar received small dues in great variety, including 2d for tithe of foals, 1d for a hive of bees, in place of tithe of honey and wax, 1d for tithe of fruit on ancient orchards and 1½d for tithe of milk on every cow.

The last major reconstruction of Kirkby Moorside Church came in 1874-5, when the noted Victorian architect, Sir Giles Gilbert Scott, supervised a major overhaul of the structure and the entire rebuilding of the chancel. The priest's part of the building now gained an emphasis that it had not had before. The chancel was given three high-pitched roofs, taller even that the embattled parapet of the nave roof, and large windows were installed which have since been filled with stained glass. On the south side, one of the old windows was taken down and merely reset, the stonework which had blocked it being removed, and the other was replaced with a replica, set in the south wall which was straightened. Much old stone was re-used here, but the cross fragments were taken out and built into the new vicarage east of the church. Most of the chancel work was carried out at the expense of the Earl of Feversham, who a few years later secured the patronage, the right to nominate priests to the living.

In the body of the Church there were other reconstructions, towards which the parishioners raised £1,200. The crowded high pews in the nave, and the gallery beneath the tower were taken out and the floor deepened. In the process several ancient graves were disturbed. D. Morris, a Kirkby emigrant to Kansas City, U.S.A., later wrote to the Vicar telling how he prevented looting of the Brooke tomb during the work. In his own words, he advised them that "if there is Gold, Silver or Jewels in that coffin, they are not ours". He also mentioned the tradition that Lady Brooke lived in the Stuteville Castle at the hilltop east of the church.

As the work was completed, a new north Chapel and a south vestry with organ chamber were added to the chancel. The north nave aisle was widened to twice its previous width, and here again at ground level, the workers had to break a great slab covering a large tomb. In the south wall, the masons themselves left a bottle containing their own names and other small items for the enlightenment of generations engaged in any future reconstruction. Next on the list for rebuilding was the Church of St. Nicholas, and St. Mary, rebuilt in 1886 at Bransdale, its dedication recalling its ancient link with Keldholme Priory. For a time after 1871, Bransdale and Farndale formed a separate parish with their own vicar. Later, St. Mary's Farndale was rebuilt and enlarged with a gallery, at the expense of the Earl of Feversham and Church Societies, but it was not completed until after the first World War. Bransdale Church was enlarged in 1934, and re-consecrated by Archbishop Temple.

In the latter years of the 19th century, and the early decades of our own, Kikby Moorside's Church and the village chapels, alongside those of the Independant, and the Primitive and Wesleyan Methodist denominations, enjoyed large congregations. Churchgoing was for a time one of the proprieties of life for respectable people. Each denomination was running its own Sunday School by 1824, where many people first learnt to read. Later National Day Schools were founded in association with the Church of England. Methodist Chapels, with Sunday Schools and classes, were established in each of the villages. Church House, Kirkby Moorside, built in 1912 provided a social centre for the town.

# Chapter Two: Rebuild and Redesign

Kirkbymoorside's All Saints Church has seen numerous alterations and rebuilds throughout its long history. Between 1183 and 1199 stone was used to create the body of the church in the Norman style but had a thatched roof. By the 1400s the thatch had been replaced with a more substantial covering however it was neglect that finally brought the church to notice. In a court roll from that period the sorry plight of the building is recorded:

*Kirkbyemoresyde "The Chancell is in great ruyne and decaye ( and hath been so vii years) both in the walles, glasse windows and leads thereof and it hath been often compleyned upon and no redresse had. They thinke that Sir Robert Constable knight fermor of the parsonage there ought to repaire the same."*

The name Constable is known to many historians as being one of those families involved with the Pilgrimage of Grace, which sought to protest at the break from the Catholic Church and which ultimately led to the execution of many. This included another Sir Robert Constable who met a gruesome death in Hull.

"*On Frydaye, beyng market daye at Hull, Sir Robert Constable suffred, and dothe hang above the highest gate of the towne, so trymmed in cheynes, that I thinke his bones will hang there this hundrethe yere.*"

In the end it was to be the Neville family who funded the restoration of the church. However after taking part in the Pilgrimage of Grace and the Rising of the North in 1569, they too were stripped of their titles and lands. The Duke of Buckingham, favourite of King Charles was the beneficiary. George Villiers, 2nd Duke of Buckingham was a larger than life character who lived life to the full.

He would later die here in Kirkbymoorside following a hunting accident without a penny of his wealth left. A record of his death is to be found in the church burial registers - *1687, April 17th, George Vilaus, lord dooke of bookingam* – although it is understood he was formally buried in Westminster.

In 1795 Mrs Dorothy Comber, wife of the Rev. William Comber, donated a parish clock which was added to the clock tower.

However a little over eight years later the tower itself had to be rebuilt. Two of the buttresses, one to the north and one in the south-facing wall were both preserved and incorporated into the new tower. In addition a parapet was erected on the top in place of the spire which was there previously. After 100 years in the tower, the state of Mrs Comber's clock was causing real concern as it could no longer be relied upon. The clock played a vital role for many of the residents who needed it in days before wrist watches were commonplace. The Kirkbymoorside Rural District Council commissioned a firm in Leeds to see what work was needed and they sent back a damning report.

*Dear Sir*

*We think the Church Tower, the best position for the clock and the dial which is the proper size, only requiring re-painting and gilding, but all the wheels and hands would have to be new, the present ones are very bad, also the hands are too thin and weak. The dial is well seen from the Market Place, which no doubt is the most important position in the town. Also the bells are very good ones, and the Church being situated on the top of the hill allows the sound of the bells to get well away all over town.*

<u>The Clock</u>, now in the tower, is about one of the worst, and weakest we ever had the pleasure of seeing, in a Church Tower. There is no maker's name on the clock that we could find out, and it appears to have been made at different periods and by different men. The old iron framework, and 2 large wheels which are of iron seem to be about 200 years old. The dial wheels seem to have been put in at a later period, also the escarpment and pendulum, the wheels are too small and light and the teeth are very badly cut, not being straight. The Pinions or small wheels that run in the larger wheels seem to have been put in by one of the last parties who had the clock in hand.

1. <u>The Frame</u> is as weak a frame as ever we saw, and this part ought to be firm and solid as possible for correct timekeeping.
2. <u>All the Bushes</u> or bearings, are fitted into the frame; consequently, if a wheel is to be taken out, you have all the clock to pull to pieces instead of unscrewing a couple of bushes, as it ought to be. Also all the bushes are worn and the holes twice as big as they should be.
3. <u>The Main Wheels</u> are thin, and badly made of wrought iron, the barrels are of wood, with hemp rope, attached and wood pulleys and stone trough of iron weights instead of thick strong main wheels, iron barrels, steel cords, iron block pulleys, brass bushes and pivoted in weights made of iron slips, like a weighing machine weights, so that you can slip one on, or off, as wanted.
4. <u>The Escarpment</u> is a bad one and likely to get bent or broken. Also it cannot keep good time, if there is a long rickety pendulum rod attached. It should have Lord Grimthorpe's gravity escapement, which is the most correct with a Compensation Pendulum attached, composed of iron and zinc tubes, with steel rod through the centre, and heavy cylindrical iron rod of cast iron. The pendulum being compensated would not be affected by the weather.
5. <u>The Maintaining</u> power is bad, and roughly made, also weak.
6. <u>The Striking</u> part of the Hours Main Wheel is a thin common wrought iron wheel with pins switted on to lift the hammer, instead of a thick strong well-made one, with a proper cam wheel attached, which lifts a heavier hammer easier, the locking plate is a thin common wheel with pins stuck in, instead of a proper striking one, with iron, and properly fitted slots, and properly fitted repeating one. The snail is a badly fitted contrivance, instead of a strong well finished one, there is no proper arrangement for setting the outside hands, nor is there any

index on the inside to let the caretaker know how to set the outside hands, which are provided.

7. <u>The present church clock</u>, although weak, worn and badly contrived, takes up double the room of a properly constructed clock, which would not be so much in the way of the Ringers as the present clock, the new clock would be easier wound up, easier looked after besides keeping more correct time, and bringing more sound out of the Bell, there would not be half the wood casing required, as at present.

8. Consequently for reasons stated above, should not recommend rickety, old fashioned piece of mechanism, having not a single redeeming feature about it, or anything about it that is worth preserving, - we would advise a modern clock, with all the latest improvements inserted that would keep time, not like the old one, as the vicar remarked, that when going it was greater trouble than standing altogether, as it mislead his choir, and mislead businessmen who had trains to catch, in fact misleading everybody.

9. We understand that you have a nucleus of £24, in hand, also several promises of help from residents and others, the Vicar also promised to throw open his grounds for a sale of work, and band performance, which we think if taken up by the Committee spiritedly, would more than cover all the expense wanted, and get a clock the Standard Timekeeper of The Town and District, which we would have no hesitation in assisting, also would supply a First Class Article Second to no other firm, and if the order was placed with us would take whatever money was in hand on completion and allow the Committee 12 months to pay the balance in, and also not make any charge for our visit and expenses yesterday, that is if we are honoured with your esteemed order.

William Potts & Sons
Clockmakers       ...
Leeds

After much debate and fundraising the Town Council placed an order for a clock in May 1894 which cost a total of £90. The mechanism is still in place today.

Another of Mrs Comber's gifts to the church interior was that of an organ which she acquired along with George and Francis Atkinson. However it did not last very long either and had to be replaced in 1820 after a candle fell into the organ during a service and set fire to it! In October 1925 work to rebuild the organ was undertaken by Wood & Wordsworth of Leeds. This would take two years to complete at a cost of £370. During that time Mr Fletcher had to play a harmonium, which was borrowed to ensure church services didn't suffer. The old organ was powered by hand bellows until 1944 when an electric blower was fitted. Many residents still recall Walter "Sunshine" Sonley who would pump the bellows by hand to ensure the organ didn't falter. The choirboys would check the weight wasn't visible through the slot – if it was then the organ would fade. Walter would stand in the vestry and so wasn't visible to many but he could be heard singing away. He was often seen rocking in time to All Things Bright and Beautiful and in between verses he would count 1, 2, 3, 4…

so as to keep the organ music constant. After 1944 Walter's in-depth knowledge of the hymns was put to good use as part of the choir itself. The organ had to be repaired again in the 1960s at a cost of £500 when dry rot was discovered underneath it, causing the whole thing to tilt forward. Whilst the organ was out of action a piano was used to accompany the choir. However time took its toll and the organ had to be replaced altogether in 1980. The plaque on it is dedicated to George Frederick Fletcher who was the organist and choirmaster for 46 years and who died in July 1942.

However it was to be Sir George Gilbert Scott who would have a lasting impact on the interior of the church. Commissioned in 1874 and funded in part by Lord Feversham, Sir Gilbert Scott set about transforming the interior of the church into the Victorian Gothic edifice we see today. During this major project church services were moved to the Toll Booth, now known as the Memorial Hall.

At a cost of £4,000 the chancel was radically altered. Plaster ceilings were removed to expose the high vaulted wooden ceilings and the high-sided box pews which each had their own coal-fired heaters made way for the more conventional pews now in place.

The roofs either side of the chancel may also be wooden but date back to the 15th Century and if you take the time to stare up at them you will find an array of carved roof bosses. There are 13 different images carved into the blocks which are hard to see, hidden in the darkness. However on one of them you can see the coat of arms of the Neville family who were the church's benefactors in the 1500s. There are also images of the Green Man in various forms – the Green Man being a symbol of rebirth and the natural cycle of life. It became a particularly popular image for the Gothic Revival era having previously lost favour for being too pagan in origin.

Temple Moore was articled to Sir George Gilbert Scott, Jr. from 1875 to 1878 and stayed with him as an assistant. He too was a devotee of the Victorian Gothic revival and this is echoed in the elaborate carvings on the choir stalls, the screen which separates the chapel and chancel and of course the pulpit. After Temple Moore left Sir Gilbert Scott's employ in 1878, he undertook commissions in his own right and would return to Kirkbymoorside church to design the chancel screen, commissioned by Harrison Holt in 1919 as a tribute to those who fell in the Great War. Temple Moore also designed the War Memorial in 1920 shortly before he died. The crucifix which hangs  above the lecturn was donated by Major A E Blythe Jackson formerly of The Green, Kirbymoorside, in thanks for his safe return from the Great War.

Much of the masonry had been re-worked previously and it is known that in 1851 workmen uncovered a wall painting of a bishop and mitre whilst repairing a window of the nave. Images such as those seen in Pickering church today would have covered the walls in Kirkbymoorside church as well. However, during the time of Cromwell and the Commonwealth of England (1649 -1658) he decreed that all traces of Catholic imagery and biblical scenes which still adorned most churches be removed in favour of a simple white interior. The painting disappeared once again under plaster after the restoration of the east window.

Some of the stonework which had been in the building since its beginning was also removed during the restoration work. Stone crosses and intricately carved lintels were rehomed in the vicarage until it was sold and the carvings were taken up to the Ryedale Folk Museum for safe storage. However at least one feature survived the rebuild, albeit in a different location. Hidden in a south facing window near the church door is a Saxon sun dial. Dating back to the 11/12th Century it is comparable in age to the one found at Kirkdale. Sadly it is badly worn and the lines which would mark the hours are only just visible but could have been part of the very first stone church on the site. Perhaps Sir Gilbert Scott inadvertantly saved one of the church's original features by bringing the sundial inside and using it in the window jamb.

The restoration wasn't unsympathetic to the past and certainly didn't try to remove all the old aspects of the church. In fact the architect replicated the original Norman window, which was still in the chancel, and installed the copy above the original 14th Century sedilia and broken piscina. Sedilia

are stone seats on the south side of an altar in the chancel, for the use of the Catholic priests and the piscina was used to drain away water used during Mass. The seats and basin are set back into the main wall of the church itself and are original to All Saints.

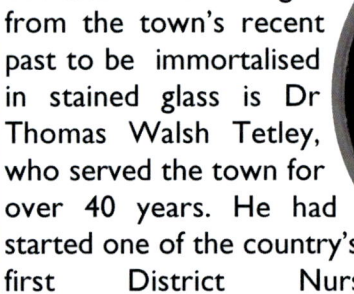

The stained glass windows in All Saints really are a true reflection of the various stages of its life.

One piece of medieval glass remains tucked away in the vestry. Perfectly framed by stone tracery "the Face of God" shines down through the centuries and is quite breath-taking when viewed close to. The memorial windows begin around 1860s. The large East Window was a gift to the church in 1908 by the Duncombe family.

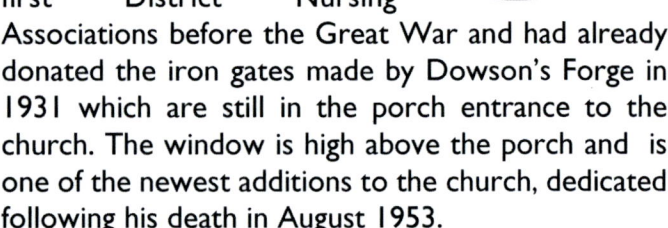

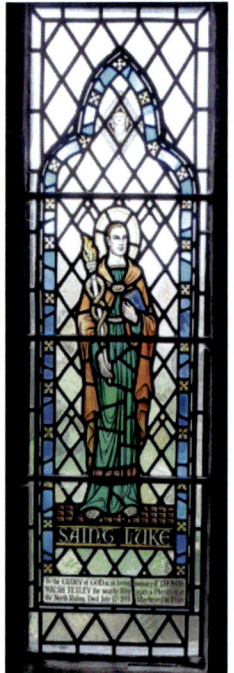

In January 1924 the wonderful round window in the tower was dedicated. Another figure from the town's recent past to be immortalised in stained glass is Dr Thomas Walsh Tetley, who served the town for over 40 years. He had started one of the country's first District Nursing Associations before the Great War and had already donated the iron gates made by Dowson's Forge in 1931 which are still in the porch entrance to the church. The window is high above the porch and is one of the newest additions to the church, dedicated following his death in August 1953.

Most of the stained glass is traditional in design and style, except for one window which is almost unique in the country. In an article written by John Hunt for the Pharmaceutical Journal, he records the story behind the family whose legacy allowed the commissioning of the pharmacy window.

Today visitors can easily see the figures of St Cuthbert and his wife Hildemar in the Lady Chapel window, but in the bottom corner the real story is revealed. A small scene showing a pestle and mortar, medicinal bottles filled with coloured liquids and Wrothwell's Chemist shop links it directly to Kirkby's history. The Wrothwells moved to the town in the 1930s and both father and son worked together in the chemist's shop, where they also sold agricultural supplies and of course liquor. This tradition is continued by the chemist's present owners, Mr & Mrs Towler, who have retained the license to drink alcohol on site. Dedicated to the memory of Frederick & Emily Wrothwell and also to that of their son Frederick Marshall who died in 1945, this window is one of very few known examples of memorials to pharmacists.

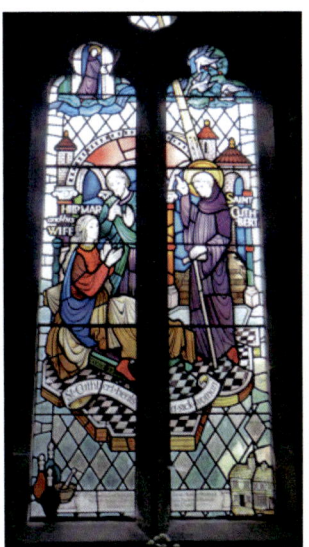

Another more recent addition to the interior of the church is a small bronze plaque remembering Mr Penn Curzon. Sherbrooke who was Master of the Sinnington Hounds for 17 yrs between 1894 - 1904. Surrounding the walls are numerous marble memorials recalling names from the town's distant past. How many people who have been into the church have looked up and seen the magnificent plaque dedicated to the memory of Mr William Bearcroft.

He is described as an untaught man of science and originated from Pockley. He ran a private school for boys in the town for many years and died in 1846. He was also a church warden and so is buried inside the church, just before the door and if you look you can still see the stone slab on the floor bearing the name Bearcroft. Other impressive marble tablets remember the Hobsons from High Hall and the Atkinson family who lived at Buckingham House where George Villiers died.

Turning to the reredos in the Lady Chapel – the almost black wooden panels date back to the Jacobean period of James I and are not original to All Saints. Research done by Eric White revealed that the panels were brought up from St Nicholas' Church in Knaptoft, which was ransacked by Cromwellian troops during the 1600s. The Lady Chapel itself was refurbished in the 1930s when the Girls' Friendly Society took on the task of raising £300 to refit the chapel. Through sales of work, dances and donations of money and items the target was achieved and on 14th July 1932 the chapel was re-dedicated by the Archbishop of York. The fifty wooden chairs, many bearing dedications, were bought at this time.

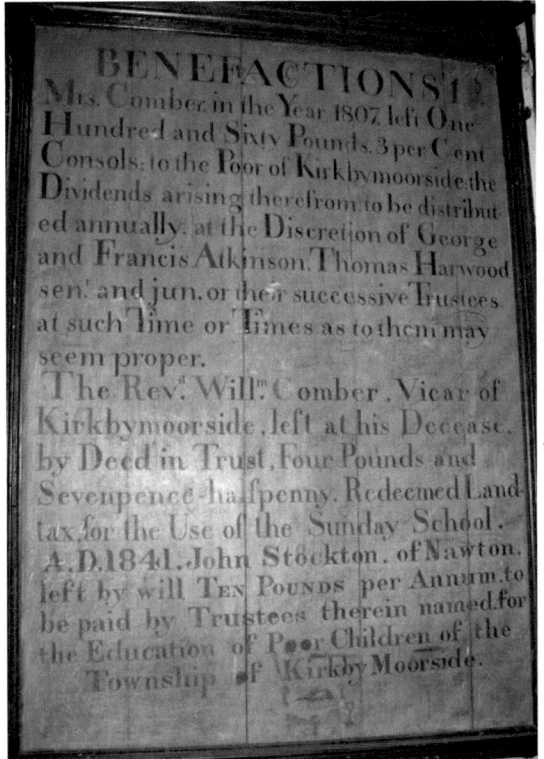

The other items of interest adorning the church walls are the Charities Boards which give information on the bequests left to the church, often with directions that the monies should be paid out to the poor and needy of the parish.

One such benefactor was John Stockton. Born in 1751 he lived and worked in Nawton, accumulating his wealth as an innkeeper and farmer. He ran the Lettered Board, which was on the site of the present-day Southfields farm and house and has an epitaph hanging in St Gregory's Minster, Kirkdale. It tells us that "..By Industry and Perseverance he acquired an ample fortune the greater part of which he bequeathed in trust to several townships, for the education of poor children."

When he died he bequeathed some of his wealth to various parishes with instructions it be used to educate the poor. In the 1800s the amount given to the needy of the parishes ranged from £5 to £15. Today the John Stockton Foundation continues that bequest and gives grants ranging from £30 to £60 to students aged 16 – 25 yrs.

The other key feature in the church itself is the impressive font. Carved from Frosterley marble, it has the following inscription around the base:

D M CUST / M A / HUJUS / ECCLESIÆ / VICARII / AD / MDCCCLXXV / E-DON-O

This relates to Rev. Daniel Milford Cust, who was vicar at All Saints from 1874 – 1877. The font was installed in 1875 during the restoration. The use of this type of marble is unusual as it is more commonly found in the monastery sites in Weardale, where the stone has been taken from the Rogerley Quarry for over 700 years. It is found in York Minster and Auckland Castle; Durham Cathedral has decorative columns made from Frosterley marble which date back to 1350 and so it is a high status piece indeed for All Saints. As well as being used for baptisms, the font is often decorated by the Sunday School for church festivals.

The marble is in fact a black limestone with a huge number of fossils visible once cut and polished. The fossils which are found throughout, are called crinoids or sea-lilies. They are like a feathery starfish perched on top of a stem which anchors the creature to the rocks.

*Decorating the font for Christmas*

*Left:: The polished marble shows the remains of the sea-lilies.*

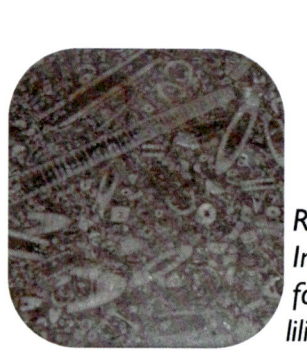

*Right: Intact fossilised sea-lilies*

In addition to the gift of the font the church pulpit was renewed and carved in the same style as the screens.

Not all gifts are so ancient. The wrought iron chandeliers which light the nave were given to the church in memory of Mr Wilf Dowson by his widow.

Up the small steps to the immediate right of the entrance is the parvise.

Originally the shelter for the priest, complete with fireplace and chimney, the sloping floor was replaced with a more usable flat surface. Providing valuable storage space, it is home to some of the bibles which have been donated over the years and are now either in need of restoration or are simply too big to be used. Some of them contain the signatures of the donors; Mr J H Dobson donated service books for the Lady Chapel in 1932 as did Dora Annie Harnby. Another more damaged bible was gifted to All Saints in 1824 by the churchwardens of the time. The bible was rebound on Ascension Day in 1889 but has since been vandalised and is no longer on view (photo aside).

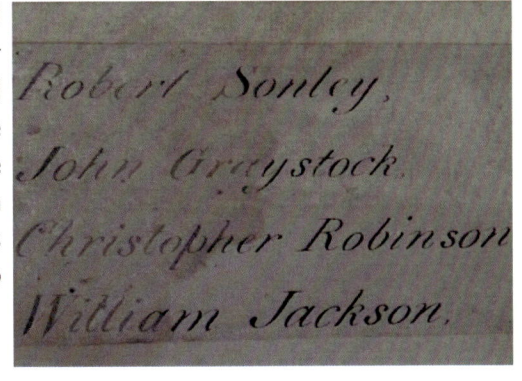

# Chapter Three: The Bells of All Saints

Many people will have heard the bell-ringers practising on a Tuesday night and no wedding would be complete without the peal of music from the tower as the bride and groom leave the church. As mentioned previously the bell tower was rebuilt in 1802 and the three bells removed. These were melted down and a set or ring of six bells made by John Taylor of Loughborough in 1803 and the tenor bell still bears the inscription "*This peal was cast 1803 Thos. Sowray, Wm Hodgson, John Masar, Wm Bearcroft Churchwardens*"

In 1936 to celebrate the birth of their son James, Captain and Mrs Vernon Holt paid for the peal to be recast by Taylors of Loughborough and the front five bells are now inscribed "*Taylors of Loughborough recast 1936*" with the tenor bell having the additional wording "*Vernon and Elizabeth Holt caused these bells to be recast and rehung in the summer of 1936 – AS Harnby Vicar, WHF Hoodless, W Rickards, Churchwardens.*" It was a delicate operation to get the six bells out through the narrow window of the tower. They were all removed on 6th July and re-dedicated on 26th November 1936.

Since then only minor work has been needed to maintain the quality of the bells. However in times past the bells were used to convey a variety of messages for the townsfolk as well as those attending the church services, messages which are no longer told or known about. In the early part of the 1900s the bells rang on Christmas Eve to tell the people it was time for the Frumenty Meal. This was a meal of stiff porridge made with cracked wheat, treacle and brown sugar spiced with nutmeg or cinnamon. The meal was taken by the whole family, often in silence with no-one allowed to leave until everyone had finished.

A more sombre occasion was marked by the bells of All Saints when the death bell was heard throughout the town. There was a very precise system in place: three tolls for a child, six for a woman and nine for a man. In addition the bell also rang out the age of the deceased, one toll for every year of their life. The practise was discontinued during WWII when the bells would be rung to signal a German invasion. However they rang out again after victory was declared in 1945.

In 2002 the deaths of Princess Margaret and later Queen Elizabeth, the Queen Mother, were marked with the bells rung half-muffled. To muffle the the bells a leather pad (the muffle) was strapped to the clapper, so if only one side is covered then the sound of the bells is deadened on alternate strokes giving them an almost echoey sound.

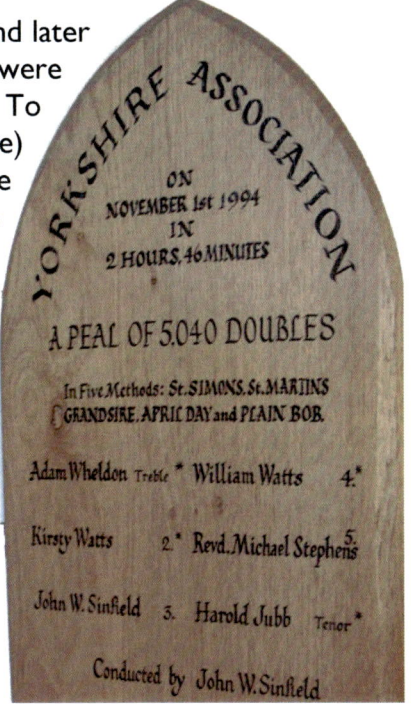

The team were also required to do a "whole pull and stand" and the bell-ringers needed a great deal of skill for this. All six bells were rung twice followed by the heaviest bell, the tenor, twice on its own. This was repeated for every year of their lives – Princess Margaret was 71, and the Queen Mother was 101. The team needed all their skills to keep control of the bells, whilst keeping the strikes accurate.

The bell-ringers or campanologists of Kirkbymoorside continue a long tradition and are dedicated to keeping the bells alive. However their predecessors were a formible act to follow.

In 1936 the newspapers reported on the longevity of one of the Kirby bell-ringing team, Arthur Wood, who had been a bell-ringer for 61 years, from 1875 to 1936. During that time he had also been in the choir for 58 years! His father before him had rung the bells for 40 years. He was not alone in his dedication to All Saints. Jack Anderson was a member for 45 years, John Rickaby for 44 years, J Harrison and Harry Masterman both served for 40 years between 1908 and 1948. When one of their own, Francis Rickaby, died in in 1934 the team marked the occasion with a muffled peal, a very special honour indeed.

From 1953 Alan Rutter was captain with long standing members such as William Spenceley and Tom Hammond. During the 1960s and 1970s Tom became captain of the bell-ringing team and was able to pass on much of the experience he had learnt from these previous stalwarts. Without that link to the past, a great deal of skill and expertise would have been lost. Through Tom, the art of English bell-ringing was passed onto the new members.

English bell-ringing is difficult as the bells swing in a full circle and are rung in "changes". Change ringing is the art of ringing a set of tuned bells in a series of mathematical patterns called "changes". It differs from many other forms of bell-ringing (such as carillon ringing) because no attempt is made to try and produce a conventional melody. Today, change ringing can be found all over the world, but it remains most popular where it developed in the 1600s, in the church towers of England. These typically contain a few large bells rigged to swing freely: a ring of bells. The considerable weight involved mean that each bell usually requires its own ringer.

In 1980 Ruth Pilmoor was captain and team members included locals Jack and Cynthia Russell. Until the 1980s these changes, or patterns, were placed on boards, which were propped up in front of the ringers, with each bell having a number and the team followed the sequence of numbers. With the arrival of John Sinfield in 1988 the team moved to "method" ringing which gave the members greater freedom and less correction by the captain.

In 1994 All Saints Church celebrated its 1200th anniversary and in honour of the occasion the bell-ringers rang a peal which took them two hours and 45 minutes. To complete a peal, the team had to ring 5040 changes of double, a formidable task and this was the first time it had been done by the local team. The occasion was marked with a peal board mounted in the bell tower.

For those who have ventured up the tiny staircase which climbs up the bell tower, the floor where the team work is called the ringing chamber and above that the bells are housed. Although there are no official records of those who have rung the bells, in the ringing chamber you will see a benefactor board. On it are recorded the bequests made by Rev. Comber to the town. However over the years many of the townsfolk who rang the bells of All Saints have signed this same board in pencil with their names and dates as a mark of their gift to the town. There is also a board commemorating the captains of the bell tower.

*Rev. Stephens, Mrs Stephens and Adam Wheldon*

Today, the team, or band as it is known, compete in many of the competitions and in recent years the Kirkby team has come 1st on five occasions, in the Annual Striking Competition, which is held between bands in the Scarborough & District Branch of the Yorkshire Assoc. of Change Ringers. The captain today is Rev. Michael Stephens and the team is always keen to hear from anyone interested in joining.

## Chapter Four: Kirkbymoorside's Choral Interest

The Kirkbymoorside & District Choral Society were the source of many a good evening's entertainment. They would regularly give grand concerts and had around 70 singers who would come together to perform in the Toll Booth. Some of the principal singers were paid performers from York and Leeds. However it would be the arrival of a certain Mr George Frederick Fletcher which would have an impact on the choir of All Saints.

Born in Scarborough in 1876, George's father managed in a draper's shop in Norwood St. His father, David, had been born at Beck Isle Pickering, where his father had been a dyer. David had learnt the drapery trade as an apprentice with a Mr Hollings at London House in Burgate, Pickering before moving to settle down in Scarborough and raise five children.

*Parish Church, KIRKBYMOORSIDE. FRIDAY, MARCH 26th, 1920, AT 7.30 P.M. STAINER'S 'Crucifixion' CHORUS of 60 Voices. SOLOISTS:— MR. WILFRID HUDSON (TENOR) MR. WILLIAM HAYLE (BASS) Silver Collection will be taken for the Music Fund. M. R. Coultman, Printer, Kirkbymoorside.*

When George returned to this area he took lodgings in Castlegate with Mr & Mrs Burton and titled himself "Professor of Music". He was an accompanist for the Choral Society in the beginning but would progress to be one of the leading

*Mr Rickaby, Wood, Anderson, Sturdy & Rutter in 1933*

musical figures in many future events. As a music teacher he would give lessons in singing and playing the piano and organ and so it was inevitable that his talents would attract the attention of the vicar. So in 1896 he became organist and choirmaster of All Saints.

The choir at All Saints had been very well supported over the years and a note found attached to the back of this photograph gives an insight into the choir during the 1880s. It shows the Kirkbymoorside Church Choir, taken outside the porch in the time of Rev. Ketchley (1877 -1905). The note states that four of the choir came from the same family; Robert, John, Frank and Tom Anderson and that the choirmaster, who sat beside Rev. Ketchley, was Mr French.

Such was the reputation of the KMS choir in those days, it says, that people would come from far away to listen and that The Green was filled with pony and traps and horses belonging to the congregation. As women were not allowed to join the choir those who wanted to sing along would sit in the front pews of the Lady Chapel. The note says that two of the girls Lily and Ethel would join in with their brothers from the sidelines.

The Anderson family can be traced back through the years. Thomas Anderson and his wife Hannah (née Cook) were both born in 1849. Thomas was born in Middleton, but moved with his parents to Chapel

Yard (these cottages no longer exist but were near the Methodist Chapel). Following his father's death, Thomas (left) moved to Howe End, into the cottage next door to Joseph Carter, and worked as a shoemaker. After his marriage to Hannah in 1871 he became the 'Rural Letters Postman' for the town and moved to Piercy End. There the couple had eight children, with all four boys part of the choir.

In those days the choir was all male and with the high numbers attending church Mr Fletcher had the pick of the boys. He would audition them and if they made the grade they would have to attend the church services. The boys would all sit together in the Lady Chapel with the girls (who could not join) waiting for a place in the choir stalls to become available.

There were 18 choirboys and two probationers in the front stalls and twelve men in the rear. As with the Andersons, father and sons would often follow one another through the years. As well as parental expectations, another incentive for the boys to join was the fact that they were paid! They received 1d for each Monday and Friday practise, and a penny for every sung service. Good behaviour attracted a further 1d. As well as cash, the choirboys received medals with bars added for every year they served, so it was easy to see the seniors. To obtain a bar the choirboy had to attend every session with no more than two absences throughout the year. One boy managed to obtain so many bars that he earned an additional 8d per week for his loyalty. All this was funded from Mr Fletcher's own pocket. These incentives along with the dedication and hard work of the boys and men ensured that the high quality of the choir was commented upon.

The boys called him "Fuzzy" Fletcher despite the fact he was always clean- shaven. However it was not all work and no play in the choir stalls.

Two local choirboys, Teddy Gulwell and Chris Boddy remember rolling up silver paper into balls and firing them at each other from one side of the choir stalls. And it wasn't only the vicar who would be watching them; they had to beware of the men sitting behind them. In Chris's case a certainly Mr Stanley Bowes would be sitting in the stall behind him and if he caught them, Stan would hit Chris on the top of the head with one of the more sturdy bibles.

The choir boys would also often be called upon by the vicar to help out with certain tasks. From 1922 to 1950 Rev. Harnby was in charge at All Saints and won the appreciation of the choirboys by ensuring they were given time off school to sing at funerals. However, he would also call on the boys' assistance in other ways. Chris recalls Rev. Harnby asking him as a young boy to climb the rickety wooden ladder in the vicarage orchard to pick apples for him, always encouraging him to reach further and further. The vicar always promised to send some apples to his mother as payment and always forgot. Robin Butler recalls he was asked by Rev. Harnby to sweep the leaves from his drive and was always paid with the foreign coins which had been put into the collection boxes. No doubt these tasks were meant as lessons in life outside the choir.

*Church Fête at Ravenswyke in the 1920s*

The choir would also go out on an annual trip in those early years, often, as was the fashion, on a charabanc to the coast or the Yorkshire Dales. However in August 1924 the choir and bell ringers went on a sightseeing trip to London where the local M.P. Sir Charles Wilson guided them round the House of Commons and the chapel. This was followed by a trip to Wembley to see the cup final – a truly memorable day for all.

Two years later there was another unusual destination for the annual trip away. In October 1926 the men and boys of the choir went to visit the port at Mr Fletcher's home town of Scarborough. There they saw the battleships HMS Hood and HMS Repulse, berthed in the harbour.

Arranged by HMS Hood's former captain, Vice Admiral Cyril Fuller who lived at Douthwaite Dale, visiting the ship was all the more poignant to those who remembered the visit in later years. In May 1941 HMS Hood encountered the German battleship Bismarck in the Denmark Strait, between Greenland and Iceland. Following heavy shelling, it was fatally damaged and sank quickly, taking with it 1415 men - only three survived.

The year after this disaster at sea, George Fletcher died on 18 July 1942 in Scarborough at the age of 66 yrs. The Rev. Canon Harnby had to step in as choirmaster and Miss L Wood took over the role of organist. Following the war and with change in society as a whole, the popularity of being choirboys declined. In 1968 All Saints decided to recruit a mixed choir. The number of girls applying outstripped the number of boys and they struggled to fill the spaces.

Today the choir at All Saints remains as dedicated as ever, albeit it in a much reduced scale to the days of Mr Fletcher. Run by Fred Dennis (see below) who is both organist and choirmaster, practise night is held on a Wednesday and Friday night from 6 pm.

Today's choir consists of
*Soprano*:
　　Margaret Bartram, Audrey Bell,
　　Barbara Scott
　*Alto*:　Dorothy Masterman, Carol Messham,
　　　　Sara Paxton, Abi Pollard
　*Tenor*:　Adam Wheldon
　*Bass*:　Warwick Bell, Les Clarke, Derrick Watson

## Chapter Five: All Saints' Church House

In the early 1900s the parish church decided to seek its own accommodation for public and private meetings in the town centre. The site chosen was north of the King's Head Hotel and two old thatched properties were demolished to make room for the new building. In 1909 the church began to raise funds in earnest as the building costs were estimated to be £1600. By 1912 £1,345 had been raised so work began and Viscount Helmsley, accompanied by his son Charles, were invited to celebrate the occasion by laying the foundation stones of the building on 29th August. The building was completed a year later.

Charles William Reginald Duncombe, 2nd Earl of Feversham (left) was known as Viscount Helmsley from 1881 to 1915. He was a Conservative Party politician and soldier, the son of William Duncombe, Viscount Helmsley. He became Member of Parliament for Thirsk and Malton in 1906 and held the seat until he inherited his title in 1915.

During WWI Viscount Helmsley fought as commander of the King's Royal Rifle Corps, which had been formed in Helmsley in 1915. Inevitably, he and his battalion were involved in the Battle of the Somme and on 15 September 1916 Viscount Feversham was killed in action at the Battle of Flers-Courcelette.

A quote from the book 'Tommy' by Richard Holmes states - "Dogs were frequent visitors to the trenches and he (Viscount Helmsley) had taken his deerhound to war: it too was killed and was buried with him" – they lay together at Flers in France, until the family had the bodies reburied at St Mary's Church, Rievaulx. His death prompted a massive sell off of land and property to cover crippling death duties and many buildings in Kirkbymoorside were bought from the Feversham Estates at the auctions on 1916.

The Church House has recently undergone a massive renovation and the original design of the building has been altered. The original layout saw one large room on the top floor with a wooden stage at one end. This room was known as the Duncombe Room and had a oak dance floor fitted which measured 20 ft by 35 ft. It was used for many events and celebrations, such as dances, wedding receptions, art exhibitions and stage productions. Especially

The wooden
**MEMORIAL CROSS**
erected under the shelter in this churchyard formerly marked the grave of Charles William Reginald DUNCOMBE, 2nd EARL of FEVERSHAM Colonel of Yeoman Rifles 21st K·R·R· killed at Flers in France and buried at the spot where he fell on September 15th 1916 during the BATTLE OF THE SOMME

Lord Feversham's body was removed from the place where it was first buried to the Cemetery at Flers and the Cross that had been made of wood from a blitzed farmhouse nearby was brought to England and placed here by his wife and by his son Charles William Slingsby Duncombe, 3rd Earl of Feversham.

popular during WWII many of the soldiers based in the camps round about would gather on a Saturday night to dance and forget for a while. Rev. Harnby was always in attendance at these events and soldiers wearing army boots were chatistized for damaging the dance floor. The last waltz was played at 11:30 pm to ensure the room was cleaned before the Sabbath. This was because during WWII evensong had to be held in Church House as they couldn't ensure the blackout in the church. For the same reason choir practise was held there too. Often the choir boys would play games and move the chairs about which prompted John Bowes the caretaker to emerge and admonish them for making too much noise. It also saw use as a magistrate's court during the war years when many buildings were taken over for the war effort. The church sexton originally had bedrooms on the upper floor which were later converted into a small kitchen area where drinks and food were prepared and served through a hatch.

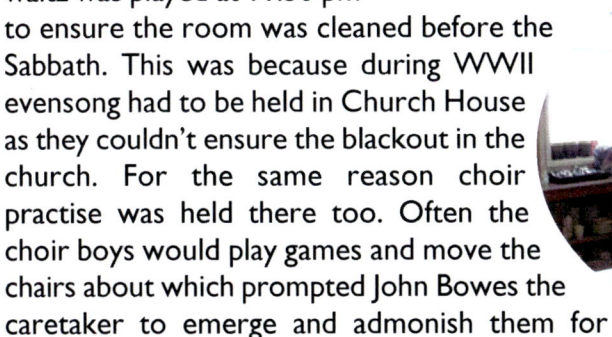

On the ground floor the building had a kitchen fitted with a cast iron range and a

*Committee room*

dumb waiter was used to get the food to the upper floor. This was removed when the new kitchen was fitted upstairs and the area became the cloakroom. The small room on the ground floor had also been used by the caretaker but was later converted for use as a committee room, where many groups could meet up including the Town Council from 1974 – 2002.

The Veteran's Billiard Club had its home in the other downstairs room. A large table donated by Harrison Holt to the men of Kirkbymoorside in 1921 dominated the room with seats fitted to the walls allowing the younger men to sit and watch the veterans play billiards. When the building was renovated in 2009, the club folded and the table was sold to a dealer in Belgium.

Another club which relied on the Church House was the Elderberry Club. It was formed around 1974 and met on a Thursday afternoon. However the flight of stone steps leading to the upper floor was too much for some. In 1988 thanks to the majority of funds being raised by the staff of the Georgian House for the Elderly in West End, an electric chair lift was fitted.

Over time repair costs mounted and the roof needed replacing. At this point NYCC were looking for a new location for the library. When Yorkshire Forward were able to match fund the project, work began to reconfigure Church House. Leased for 60 years and at a cost of around £700,000 the Learning, Library and Customer Services Centre opened its doors in September 2009. The ground floor now houses the books and public access computers. In addition staff deal with district council enquiries. The staircase leads to an upper floor which is divided into an IT suite on one side and a meeting room on the other. A lift has also been installed to allow access for all.

The two Rolls of Honour which list townsfolk from Kirkbymoorside, who were serving in WWI, originally hung on the walls of the billiard room downstairs. Restored and reframed they now hang in the new committee room upstairs – a link between the old and the new.

# Chapter Six: Churchyard and the Memorials

The churchyard surrounding All Saints is now seen as a community space as well as the burial ground. The area in the front of the church has the oldest memorial stones in it, many of them standing proud despite the years of weathering and change. Some of the graves have lost their iron railings over the years and some graves have had to be removed, but little else has altered since the late 1800s. The path which leads from Church Street is worn and hollowed out and gives the visitor a real sense of all those who have gone before.

The most noticeable memorial is the gothic tomb in front of the church. Erected in memory of Harriett Searwin, she was the wife of William Searwin from York. She died at the age of 34 and was buried on 17 January 1846. The tomb is now a listed monument and the inscription around it has become illegible due to ongoing repairs. There may also have been two angels in the niches at either end, but today they stand empty.

The oldest tombs in the churchyard are the table tombs near to the entrance. The most legible is erected to the memory of John Foxton of Keldholm which dates from 1747.

The tomb nearest to the porch is dedicated to the Atkinson family, who were the tenants of Buckingham house where George Villiers died following his accident. Their details are listed on the marble plaque inside the church. This tomb was damaged in 2010 and had to be reconstructed. Other families were wealthy enough to have their plaques placed onto the outer walls of the church itself. In an effort to preserve them lead has been added to the top edges to try and limit water damage.

Another unusual marker, which used to be found in the churchyard, was that belonging to the two infant sons of Christopher and Mary Carter. Made from cast iron it is a fabulous example of intricate casting and was done by the forge belonging to the children's father in Piercy End.

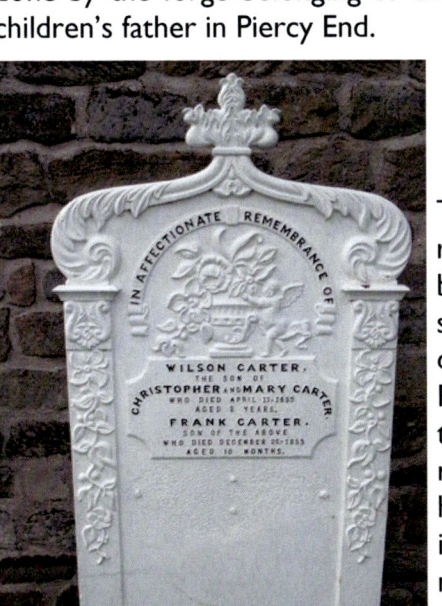

The marker was in danger of being removed as the huge slab of iron had been shattered and the protruding supports and edges were extremely dangerous. So after discussions with Rev. David Purdy and members of the family, the decision was taken to remove the marker, including the huge sandstone block which held it in place. With the assistance of members of the local history groups, the marker was relocated and rebuilt near to the forge at the Ryedale Folk Museum, repainted in its original colours, for everyone to see.

The sundial outside the entrance is set on a stone plinth and is protected by iron railings. However a photograph of the church exterior before Sir Gilbert Scott's alterations in 1875 shows the sundial in situ. It was almost certainly there before the church clock was installed in 1795. The weeping ash has grown considerably over the years and now shades both the sundial and screens the church clock for many, but has become an iconic symbol of the churchyard itself.

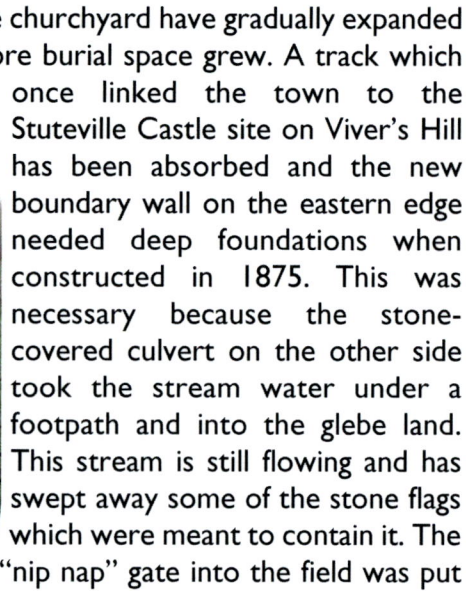

One of the stone gateposts at the entrance to Crown Square has been carved to show the date of 1767 and has remained untouched. However the size of the site within has changed. The boundaries of the churchyard have gradually expanded over the years as the need for more burial space grew. A track which once linked the town to the Stuteville Castle site on Viver's Hill has been absorbed and the new boundary wall on the eastern edge needed deep foundations when constructed in 1875. This was necessary because the stone-covered culvert on the other side took the stream water under a footpath and into the glebe land. This stream is still flowing and has swept away some of the stone flags which were meant to contain it. The "nip nap" gate into the field was put in at the same time as the wall was built. The next extension in 1907 meant the churchyard expanded into land known as the Applegarth or Apple Yard. The need for space continued and two more areas of land were taken up in 1935. The wall built between the old glebe land and the churchyard had to be well constructed, as there was a drop of about 12 feet onto the level field below. However over the years spoil was deposited over the wall into the glebe land and today there is a slope from the stonewall down to the stream. The churchyard we see today was set in 1984 and is still open for burials.

The area at the very top of the site, through the two wooden gates forms the cemetery owned and controlled by the Town Council. Howard Morley was the town clerk who saw this project through to completion, including the purchase of the one acre plot from Ravenswyke Estate. The footpath which ran across the field had to be diverted and the new boundary is marked with a beech hedge, similar to the one in the churchyard. The soil depth is not enough to allow anything other than single graves. The cemetery has areas for cremations in the bottom right-hand corner, as well as a non-consecrated section for other religions or non-religious burials in the bottom left. These areas are still unused. The cemetery itself has needed enlargement, so recently the whole site was landscaped to cope with the increasingly ageing population and the need for plots in traditional burials.

All this leads to the continuing problems of maintaining the

*Mozzotti memorial in the wildlife area*

churchyard and cemetery. Fashions have affected the designs of memorials and graveyards – gone are the iron railings and heaped graves which stood proud of the ground. Magnificent table tombs are no longer within the pockets of most residents and height restrictions and planning regulations discourage anything other than the smaller headstones. Health and safety issues have also led to unstable or weakened headstones being laid flat to prevent injury or accidents.

Within All Saints churchyard the decision to remove the kerbstones which had marked the boundary edges was made in the late 1960s under the Rev. Michael Wright. All removed kerbs were recorded in a register and then recycled, many being used by local builders. Some of the older enclosed graves had the iron railings removed at the same time. The removal of kerbstones continued in the 1980s under Rev. Hughes and today kerbs are not permitted. They were removed partly to try and keep the churchyard manageable. Grass cutting became increasingly difficult with the variety of obstacles around the churchyard and weeds were able to grow in-between the kerbs and railings. The grass is now cut on a contract basis with the local Town Council giving grants to assist with the cost of maintenance of the churchyard areas, as well as the cemetery.

In 2011 a programme of clearing many of the trees was undertaken and the north-east corner has been allowed to revert to a wildlife area to control costs. The spoil heaps in both the cemetery and churchyard have been levelled and relocated. Back in 1929 the Rev. Willson was calling upon parishioners to help keep the tower free from ivy and to wash the clock-face. Over eighty years later the church continues to rely upon the volunteers who maintain the grounds today.

Another key feature of the churchyard is the War Memorial. Designed by Temple Moore with the names carved by local masons, the area is always kept in good order by volunteers and members of the Kirkby In Bloom group.

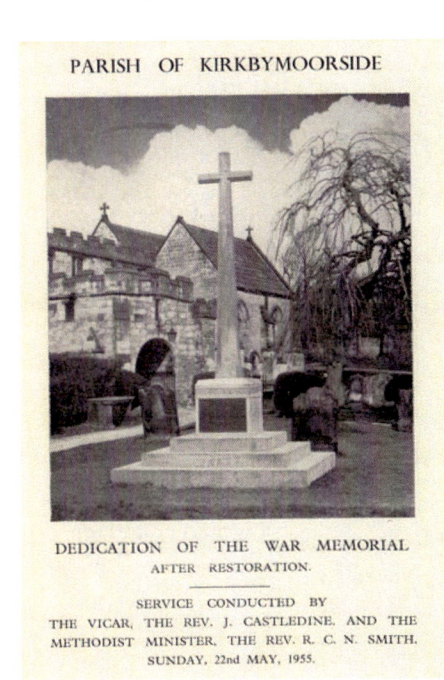

PARISH OF KIRKBYMOORSIDE

DEDICATION OF THE WAR MEMORIAL
AFTER RESTORATION.

SERVICE CONDUCTED BY
THE VICAR, THE REV. J. CASTLEDINE, AND THE
METHODIST MINISTER, THE REV. R. C. N. SMITH,
SUNDAY, 22nd MAY, 1955.

Following WWII a metal plaque with eight more names was added to the stone base. The war memorial is still well attended on Remembrance Day when the names of all those who died in service of their country are read aloud and poppy wreaths laid.

The brass plaques in the Memorial Hall listing all the men of the town involved in the Great War were dedicated on Christmas Day 1927 by Rev. Willson. They were his gift to the town.

*Left: One of three wrought iron memorial seats; renovated and repainted, it overlooks the town from Viver's Hill*

That gift was followed up many years later when a second plaque, detailing the eight men from the town who died in WWII. It was dedicated at a service held on the 22nd May 1955, conducted by Rev. John Castledine. In 2010 the three wrought iron seats, commissioned by the Town council to commemorate these men, were renovated and plaques added.

Connected with the church is the town bier. Last used in the 1930s the bier had been left in storage under the old library and had suffered very badly from damp and neglect. In 2009 the Town Council agreed to give the bier on long term loan to the Ryedale Folk Museum, where it has been restored to its former glory by one of the volunteers John Nicoll. The bier is basically a hand drawn trolley with wheels bound with Hessian rope to muffle the sound of the coffin being brought into church. It could be used by any of the townsfolk and one of the last people known to have made their final journey to the churchyard on the bier was Mrs Butler.

# LIST of VICARS

|  |  |
|---|---|
| 14 April 1288 | William de Hexhildesham |
| | Walter de Newton |
| | John Dysworth |
| 30 April 1392 | Roger de Ripon |
| 15 Nov: 1412 | John de Raskell |
| 24 Oct: 1433 | Robert Carvell |
| 24 July 1450 | Thomas Kirkby ~ |
| | *Canon and Prior of Newburgh* |
| 5 April 1484 | Nicholas Wyspyngton ~ |
| | *Canon of Newburgh* |
| 23 Aug: 1487 | Job Donald |
| 7 Feb: 1501 | Thomas Pereson vel Persay |
| 8 Jan: 1504 | William Baker |
| 16 Mar: 1505 | Thomas Weldon |
| 1 Mar: 1533 | Robert Thorp |
| | William Barker |
| 15 Dec: 1548 | Richard Judson |
| 27 Mar: 1593 | Richard Clarke M.A. |
| 27 Jan: 1594 | William Denton B.A. |
| 2 July 1619 | Henry Thurscroff M.A. ~ |
| | *Archbishop's Chaplain* |
| 28 May 1625 | Timothy Thurscroff M.A. |
| 17 Oct: 1638 | Thomas Strother M.A. |
| 12 Nov: 1660 | Thomas Harwyke |
| 5 Oct: 1677 | Thomas Shepherd |
| 1 April 1707 | James Musgrave M.A. |
| 1 Sept: 1714 | Henry Maunder B.C.L. |
| 4 Feb: 1756 | William Comber M.A. |
| 4 Mar: 1811 | Joseph Smyth B.A. |
| 11 April 1826 | Edmund Gray M.A. |
| 11 Mar: 1851 | John Rowlandson M.A. |
| 9 Aug: 1856 | Charles Rae Hay |
| 7 June 1858 | William Drayton Carter M.A. |
| 1866 | John Spencer |
| 1868 | Edward Mourant Birch B.A. |
| 7 May 1874 | Daniel Mitford Cust M.A. |
| 17 Mar: 1877 | Walter Guy Ketchley |
| 10 June 1905 | Herbert Edward Willson M.A. |
| 2 Mar: 1922 | Anthony Simpson Harnby B.A. ~ |
| | *Canon of York* |
| 29 Sept: 1950 | Albert Robinson B.A. |
| 12 June 1955 | John Castledine A.K.G |
| 5 July 1963 | Dennis Ralph Brandon B.A. |
| 26 Feb: 1968 | Michael John Wright |
| 25 July 1974 | Lionel Philip Clare |
| 7 June 1984 | Alan Ffughes |
| 15 July 1995 | David Purdy B.A.,M.Phil. |

# Chapter Seven: The Vicars and the Vicarage

A full list of vicars dating back to 1288 was written out by Helen Pierson and hangs in the church.

Positions within the church were often seen as a career for second sons, losing their claim to family estates to their older brothers who inherited the family wealth. The gift of the position of parish priest lay with the lords of the manor but as the church hierarchy evolved, control of appointments came within their domain. For the parish priest in Kirkbymoorside it was the Bishop of Whitby who had a far greater say in his appointment rather than the patron.

The current patron is Lady Clarissa Collin, (portrayed here in her position as High Sheriff of Yorkshire) and the living for All Saints Church is in her gift. Incomes in the past came from the surrounding parishes in the form of tithes and the wealth of the vicars varied widely. Some had a lot of income, land and parishioners, others were very poor indeed. Here at All Saints, the vicar would receive three types of tithes:

- praedial tithes – these were based on income from produce;
- mixed tithes - these were based on the income from stock and labour;
- personal tithes – these were based on income from labour alone

The systems used for calculating the money due to the church were complex and relied on tithe maps where all fields were marked and tenants named. The names changed frequently but the maps show that many of the fields south of the town were used to grow flax throughout the 1800s. In an attempt to simplify this for the tenants, a system of fixed rent charges was introduced in 1836 which did away with all these

*Rev. Wm Comber*

assessments. By the 1900s many of these tithe payments were removed completely by paying an agreed lump sum. In 1913 the vicar at All Saints was receiving £310 in tithes, he also had ninety acres of glebe land scattered throughout the parish and the large imposing vicarage east of the church. Much of the land had come into his predecessor's control following the enclosures of the common lands in 1796.

*Opening in 2000. L to R Rev. Purdy Harry Rickaby John Bowes Cllr David Cussons Barbara Clark and Mayor Tony Clark*

*Photo by David Ireland*

In Kirkbymoorside, the Rev. Comber gained 21 acres and 33 perches of this 'glebe' land which he could use to let out to provide him an income. The last remaining piece of glebe land to be sold became the Millennium Garden which was opened in 2000 by the Mayor Tony Clark, Rev. David Purdy and long-standing resident Harry Rickaby.

*Mosaic Panels*

The children from the school created mosaic panels which are inset into the ground and the site has been left natural although it has been used for various band concerts over the years.

The vicars of All Saints have all left their mark either in word or deed. The Rev. Edmund Gray left behind not only the chalice and loving cup he presented but also his words. A small hard-backed booklet printed by Robert Cooper contains two sermons preached in the Parish Church of Kirby Moorside on 27 March 1836. The topic of these sermons was "the due observance of the Lord's Day," and they are prefaced by the following:

> To the inhabitants of Kirby Moorside
> The following Sermons were prepared of the pulpit without the most distant idea of printing them: but the importance of the subject upon which they treat has led me to wish to place it even in the most unworthy form before those of my parishioners whom I cannot address from the pulpit: I also should wish those who may have heard the Sermons delivered, to call to mind the duty which rests upon them of keeping holy the Sabbath, by occasionally referring to the printed discourses.

*The present seems to be a time when Ministers of Christ, and their hearers, are called to make peculiar exertions for the better observance of the Lord's Day; lest, from the increasing desecration of it our Country should be visited by God with His heavy judgement; - and particularly lest He should allow infidelity, - laxity in religious opinions, - and false doctrines to increase and prevail in the Land.*

*With my earnest wishes and prayers for your welfare both in this world and that which is to come; -*

*I am, Your affectionate Minister and Friend, Edmund Gray.*

What effect this booklet had is hard to say, what is true is that church attendance has continued to decline and today the congregation has fewer younger members than ever before. Rev. Gray stayed at All Saints for 25 years and a small brass plaque to his memory can be found high on the wall near to the vestry.

His successor was the Rev. John Rowlandson who had previously served the church out in India. John was born in 1811, the son of the Rev. Michael Rowlandson, Vicar of Warminster. He studied at Queen's College, Oxford, and graduated in 1840, before serving in India under Bishop George Spencer.

Bishop Spencer had taken charge of the Madras Diocese in 1838 and he ordained several Methodist and Congregationalist missionaries during his time in office. He felt that India needed missionaries to convert the locals; in a letter written in August 1844, the Bishop wrote to London saying he had "about fifty missionary clergymen of the Church of England, and about fifty millions of heathen."

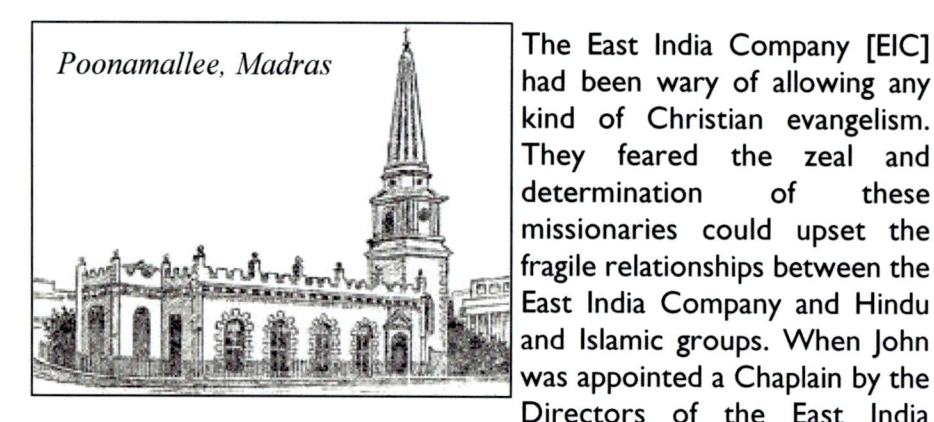

*Poonamallee, Madras*

The East India Company [EIC] had been wary of allowing any kind of Christian evangelism. They feared the zeal and determination of these missionaries could upset the fragile relationships between the East India Company and Hindu and Islamic groups. When John was appointed a Chaplain by the Directors of the East India Company in 1840 he faced not only hostile living and working conditions but also the fact that Christianity was seen as a mark of colonial rule. Nevertheless John served at Poonamallee from 1840 to 1844, and then in Quilon from 1844 to 1847. Dysentry, cholera, malaria and typhus were all common diseases and the chances of anyone living in the subcontinent without falling ill was very poor. In 1847 John fell ill and would not return to India again. In 1851 he became vicar of Kirkbymoorside and died in 1856 at his vicarage. Records show that both he and his brother George were popular in society owing to their charming manners. Indeed his memorial plaque in the church records that although *"weak and suffering in body but singularly able vigorous and energetic in mind"* he fulfilled a *"short but effective ministry of five years."* He was only 45 when he died. His brother George was Major-General Rowlandson, Commander of the Royal Madras Artillery. Like his brother he too died young at the age of 56.

*Quilon church in early 1900s*

Walter Guy Ketchley took over the incumbency in 1877 and made his mark on the parish by building the large stone vicarage which stands to the east of the church. Previous vicars had lived in the large vicarage which stood at the top of Tinley Garth (now a house) but Rev. Ketchley decided to move closer to the church and was provided with this six acre site by William Bland. He moved into the vicarage in September 1878 and in the beautifully laid out grounds he planted a Wellingtonia or giant sequoia. The tree is still growing and will remain as a memorial to him for many more years – the largest example of this tree is "the General Sherman" in USA thought to be 3,200 years old.

The interior was large and imposing but had to be lit by candles and lamps. The ancient stones taken from the church during the restoration stood on display in and around the porch until 1970. He also oversaw the planting of the beech hedge to mark the boundary of the churchyard to the east in 1879 and lamented the loss of trees planted to celebrate Queen Victoria's Golden Jubilee in 1887, thanks to some mischievous children. Rev. Ketchley created the church magazine in 1892 in conjunction with his son, Harry, who was vicar at Barton-le-Street. The four-page magazine had news of both parishes for the first few years before the link was cut. Two sons of Rev. Ketchley, Harry and Walter went on to marry two daughters of the Petch family, which ensured the families remained linked with the town through relatives who lived in Howe End. In his will he left the parish the large vicarage he had built along with the gardens and orchard. There is still a stone sundial in the grounds of the new vicarage today, which carries his name and the date 1833.

When the Rev Harnby took over from Rev Willson in 1922, he decided to develop the magazine and under his care it grew in size and detail. Initially funded by subscriptions the magazine included news from the town's events, parish calendars and even the Diocesan newsletter. Local tradesmen began to advertise and it became increasingly popular. News from St Aidan's at Gillamoor had been included from the start, but from 1941 it included St Michael's at Great Edstone. During the war years the magazine had to reduced dramatically as rationing forced paper shortages everywhere. The church magazines give a wonderful insight to the key events in the town and how the vicar saw life changing around him. During the 1940s the curate who assisted Rev. Harnby was Rev. O'Brien.

Rev. Willson

In 1953 Rev. John Castledine took up the post at All Saints. He oversaw the joining of the Bransdale and Farndale parishes with those of Kirbymoorside and Gillamoor. With fewer people coming into the church ministry, falling numbers in the congregation and rising costs, it was inevitable that the smaller parishes would eventually have to

Rev. Harnby visiting the Adela Shaw Hospital

merge. As the workload increased the need for another curate led to the appointment of Rev. Philip Garnett in 1955. However many people will remember Rev. Castledine for his work with the scouts and his wife was the Guide Captain for the 1st Kirbymoorside Girl Guides.

Rev. Michael Wright arrived at All Saints in 1968. He had been a journalist before joining the church and brought with him a very different style. He re-arranged the magazine to become much more current and also joined in with the campaign to try to halt the closure of the Adela Shaw Hospital, travelling down to London to protest. However at the same time he became the centre of the ensuing debate over the location of the health centre which was proposed to replace the services lost from the Adela Shaw. The conflict came when Drs Cooke & Williamson refused to work at the health centre unless it was built adjacent to their surgery, located in The Green. They wanted the centre to be build in parts of the vicarage orchard.

*Rev. Michael Wright*

Rev. Wright wanted this area of land to build a new vicarage, the large stone property was proving too costly to run. Battle lines were drawn and no agreement could be reached. In 1970 the Adela Shaw Hospital shut down and the former doctors residence "Rahane" became the base for the residual services such as physiotherapy. In 1972 the new vicarage was built in the former

*Former surgery on The Green*

orchard and the large vicarage sold off as a private house.

Until recently the post of vicar had been in interregnum after Rev. Canon David Purdy (below) left in 2009. In addition to being vicar of All Saints since 1991, he was appointed honorary Canon for Langtoft before moving to a position in Hawkser cum Stainacre.

The Church still has two churchwardens – currently Liz Garthwaite and Bridget Gillespie. The parish can no longer support a curate so assistance comes from the retired clergy who live in the area. Whilst a vicar may retire, they remain priests for life and many welcome the opportunity to assist the church where possible. During the time All Saints has been without a vicar, the Rev. Canon Francis Hewitt and the Rev. Michael Stephens have often been called upon to take services.

*Left: Canon Francis Hewitt with Liz Garthwaite and Bridget Gillespie*

The new vicar of All Saints (pictured below with his family) was appointed in August 2011 – Rev. Mark Brosnan was previously vicar at St Barnabas in Hadleigh, Essex. He began at the end of January 2012 having moved up to Kirkbymoorside with his wife Tania. During his ministry he worked as a psychiatric nurse before becoming a full-time priest. Tania is a mammographer as well as an ordained Methodist Minister.

The role of finding the next vicar was one of the tasks which fell on members of the PCC. Before 1921 the churchwardens and vicar met at vestry meetings, where church business was conducted. Meticulous records were kept and here are some of the details discussed at those early meetings, although vestry meetings were not always held in a vestry. On 14 April 1851 it was decided to hold meetings in the school rooms at the foot of the steps into Church Street.

The churchwardens saw to the running and maintenance of the church, its infrastructure and day to day function. Until 1868 they had the power to levy and collect a rate from every parishioner, whether attendee of the church or nonconformist. The two or four wardens held office for one year. One, called the vicar's warden, was appointed by the vicar whilst the other was elected at a vestry meting held annually in October. The rate that they levied came to 9d in the pound rate in 1813, raising £59 ; in 1814 this was dropped to a 5d rate bringing in only £38. As a result of these widely differing amounts  objections were raised concerning the proper valuation accorded to properties in town. So in 1815 Thomas Hornby of Wombleton and George Peirson of Beadlam Grange were appointed as independent assessors.

The provision of stoves and coals to heat the church was discussed in October 1814 but was adjourned without  decision. A month later subscriptions were requested to cover heating costs. The stoves and pews would be removed in the 1874/5 refurbishment. Prior to that it had been possible to reserve the box pews for family worship. In 1817 Christopher Robinson and William Bearcroft (headmaster) paid £1/11/6d for a seat in the corner of the south aisle. In 1828 the north gallery was fitted with seats and pews rented out as follows-

| | |
|---|---|
| Mrs Surr, of Keldholme Priory | No. 2 |
| John Pilmoor | No. 4 |
| John Hugill | No. 6 |
| John Shepherd, of Douthwaite Hall | No. 7 |
| Robert Shepherd | No. 8 |

In July 1825 there was an altercation between the wardens and the team of bell-ringers. The bell-ringers had taken away and sold a number of old bell ropes keeping the profit towards some ale. In response the wardens withheld their annual payment of 10/-. The organist was more highly paid. His salary, in 1828 went up from £4/4/0 to £8. Pressure of correspondence in 1829 caused the vestry meeting to employ a vestry clerk, William Jackson, at a cost of £5 per annum.

From 1921 Parochial Church Councils (PCC) took the place of Vestry Meetings and became regulated as to their roles and responsibilities. The PCC consists of the clergy and churchwardens of the parish, together with a number of representatives of the town who have been listed on the parish roll for at least six months and then elected at the Annual Parochial Church Meeting. The vicar is the chairman of the PCC and a lay member is appointed vice-chairman. The PCC must meet at least four times a year and is responsible for the financial affairs of the church and the care and maintenance of the church fabric and its contents. At All Saints local resident Anne Warriner is currently the secretary of the PCC and has been involved at All Saints for many years.

Examples of the Church Council's work in maintaining the church include the project under the Rev. Alan Hughes (left) to replace the roof in the Sanctuary, Chancel, Lady Chapel and Vestry. A brass plaque recording the restoration work in 1991 is to be found in the chancel. The PCC were also involved in a more long term project which came to fruition in 2000. At the Crown Square entrance to the churchyard there were originally two stone properties which by 1943 were becoming an issue. The buildings were in need of extensive repair and so in Nov 1943 the PCC decided to purchase them. It took another 10 years before they were demolished at a cost of £250 and a shed erected to store tools, coke and other bulky items. However it wasn't until 2000 that the new building, which now stands at the entrance, was completed. Part of it houses much needed office space for paperwork and printing to take place whilst the other section offers toilet facilities during service times for the congregation of All Saints.

*Above: New church office and toilet block*

*Left: Original gatepost from 1767*

*Right: Mrs Dora Collier and Miss Emeline Todd retired from church cleaning duties after many years of service. Both women were regular supporters of church events. Photo: Malton Gazette & Herald*

# Chapter Eight: Sunday School and the Junior Church
*by June Cook*

It is not known when All Saints' Sunday School, now called Junior Church, was formed but it could be over 200 years ago.

The aim was to teach the poor children, who worked in industry and service, and the only time they had free was on a Sunday. The primary desire was to teach them to read and write, as only the wealthier could afford to educate their children and then often only the boys would go away to boarding school. As the movement grew the children were taught not only to read and write but also some basic religious education.

Robert Raikes (right) was the editor of the *Gloucester Journal* and one of the leading figures in the Sunday School movement. He died in 1811 and by that time the movement had spread country wide. Any child between the age of 5 and 14 was allowed to go and often the lessons would be given by ladies, who were of good standing and suitable character.

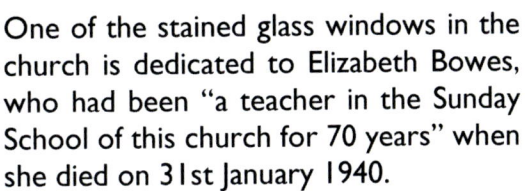

One of the stained glass windows in the church is dedicated to Elizabeth Bowes, who had been "a teacher in the Sunday School of this church for 70 years" when she died on 31st January 1940.

An elderly resident recalls that her late husband attended Sunday School in the church on a Sunday afternoon - this was around 1917 - 1920. With the building of the Church House, it was decided to move the children and the school there. At that time it was led by the two Miss Woods, Margaret and Eva and they continued until the 1960s. They lived in High Market Place and their father had a woodwork shop. They would wear cloche hats, an irresistible temptation for one boy who sought to tip it over Miss Wood's eyes during one long service in church! After they finished various people have kept the Sunday School going.

*Kirbymoorside Parish Church*

*Mothering Sunday*

This card brings greetings to the parents of all our Sunday School children, and an invitation to *The Family Service* to be held on Sunday, March 4th at 2-30 p.m.

I first became involved and took my children, Helen and John, in the early 1970s. Mrs Wright, the vicar's wife at the time was running Sunday School with Mrs Hill. Lots of people have helped over the years - Mrs Collier, Mrs Rolling and her two daughters, Mrs Thomson and Mrs Hugill to name but a few. Most came to help with and bring along their children, then stayed for several years until their children were confirmed.

In the past we had large numbers at one time 30 children, but these numbers have declined. We always gave a Christmas Party in Church House or the church, and performed other musical presentations. There was always an outing or picnic for the children in the summer.

In past years it was a trip to Scarborough or Filey on a coach or by train when the station was still open in Kirkbymoorside. This has now ceased as most people go off on their own and family holidays are the norm.

Today Sunday School takes place on a Sunday 10 - 11 am in the Dugout, as the Church House is leased to the NYCC as a library.

*Above: Sunday School Picnic*

At 11 am we join the main service for the Communion, enabling the leaders and children to take part and even tell the congregation what activities they have done. On the second Sunday each month we join the All Age Service in the Church. The helpers are parents and friends of the children, and we have three leaders who work on a rota basis. All those who work with the children are screened by the police and undergo CRB checks. All ages of children attend from 4 to 11 years of age. A warm welcome is extended to any child in the area.

At the age of 11-12 years children can go to confirmation classes held by the vicar. Confirmation candidates attend a series of special classes to learn about the sacrament, the faith and their Christian responsibilities.

*Confirmation candidates (above) in 1969 and (right) in 2000*

Confirmation preparation helps candidates to have a proper understanding of how to live as a follower of Christ. At one time, candidates were required to learn a series of questions and answers by heart known as the catechism. Today's classes are more comprehensive and the particular needs of candidates will be borne in mind. Often children would go in groups to be confirmed at All Saints.

Another tradition which is no more - the giving of Sunday School prizes. Regular attendance was always encouraged and, in the early years, books were given to those earning enough marks. Many a bookcase holds an early example of these prizes, often tales of religious courage or trial. By the 1970s children would collect religious stamps to fill an album in order to receive their prize.

# Chapter Nine: The Church Of Today

The Church of All Saints was previously involved in community life to a much greater extent than it is today. It was unthinkable at one time to not invite the vicar to bless an opening of a major building or event. When the new tennis pavilion opened in July 1929 Rev. H Willson presided. With the changing attitudes in society the church's role has been diminished, but here in Kirkbymoorside three different churches come together to celebrate key events. The churchyard is shared for burials and at Christmas there is the Journey to Bethlehem. Each year one of the churches organises the procession around town where the Christmas story unfolds and carols are sung. There is usually a donkey to carry Mary and the journey ends at the Methodist schoolroom for warming refreshments.

*Sisters Melissa & Heather Mudd guided by their dad ride Max in the arctic weather of 2010*

Visitors to All Saints at Christmas are also welcome to join in with the Christingle Service where the children receive an orange decorated with sweets and a red ribbon. These represent the world and the seasons, with the ribbon symbolising God's love for all. Into the orange a candle is inserted and this is lit during the service from the Pastoral Candle. The effect within the church is enhanced by the sandstone pillars. The crib service on the 24th December is also lit by candlelight and children make their way to the altar to see the nativity. There were over 200 candles distributed at the service in 2011.

At Easter the crucifix is carried from Church House to All Saints in the Palm Sunday procession. One of the now forgotten Easter traditions involved the rolling of eggs down the hills above the playing fields at Howe End on Low Sunday, the Sunday after Easter. Children would spend hours staining them with onionskins or cochineal before decorating them with patterns and symbols. If a snowdrop was wrapped inside the onionskins it would leave its image on the shell. Once the eggs had been rolled down to the bottom they could be eaten. The symbolic message behind this relates to the rolling away of the stone from the tomb. That is why the parish magazines tell of the hundreds of eggs sent to hospitals from the church communities at this time of year.

As well as the services the church is made all the more inviting by the dedicated army of flower arrangers who ensure the building always looks its best. In 2010 All Saints held a flower festival with colourful displays representing patron saints and those who are in their care. 2011 saw a display of cribs within the church and over the years All Saints has hosted a great many events, from exhibitions to concerts.

At harvest-time the font and the church is dressed with fresh produce and flowers donated by the congregation. The produce is later auctioned or handed to good causes. In the past this often meant a trip down to the Yorkshire Children's Hospital later the Adela Shaw, which relied upon such good will to maintain a healthy diet for the sick children especially in the early years.

*Photo: David Ireland*

Remembrance Day always brings the focus of the town onto All Saints, where the war memorial is located. The parade begins at the British Legion Club and marches up Tinley Garth and down to Chisholm's monument, before turning into Church Street and gathering around the cross. Led by the band many representatives from various groups as well as veterans come together to pay their respects to the fall of all wars.

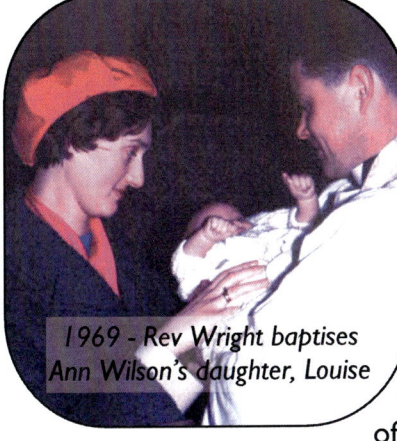

In addition to the traditional baptisms, weddings and funerals, All Saints has been involved in many charitable causes over the years; natural disasters, charities and church maintenance have all been worthy recipients of the community's donations. In recent years the church has been site of a charitable sleep-out in aid of SASH, who help homeless teenagers. Participants from all parts of the town build shelters and sleep outside in the cold for one night to raise funds. The youngest to take part was only 5 years old and the cubs often take part as a group. Each Christmas the church also donates gifts for shoe boxes which go to children sponsored by Children In Distress, a charity caring for disabled and sick children in Eastern Europe. The besom co-ordinates the distribution of food items around Ryedale to those identified as in need at Christmas and the Junior Church members appealed for contributions in 2011.

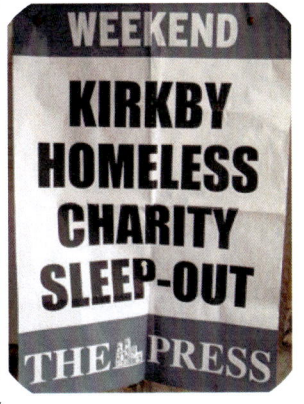

*1969 - Rev Wright baptises Ann Wilson's daughter, Louise*

The Church tradition is Central. The Worship in all four churches is centred around the Eucharist. The altar at All Saints has frontals for all the liturgical seasons. Vestments are worn at every service with a chasuble at the Eucharist; a scarf and hood are worn occasionally. The choir, crucifer, acolytes and servers are robed and are always at the main Eucharist service at All Saints. There is a procession at the start of every service and at the end.

After services volunteers offer tea, coffee and biscuits. This allows members of the congregation to meet informally and encourages greater interaction. In years gone by church outings took place annually and the large church fêtes were pivotal events in the town's social calendar. In today's busy world there is less time for organising and attending such events. Instead smaller coffee mornings and fairs are hosted by individuals at various times throughout the year.

The Mothers' Union is an international Christian charity that seeks to support families worldwide. The banner seen here was designed by Pat Staff and made by Vera Fairlamb members. It was dedicated in May 1999. The Mothers' Union also donated the wooden screen next to the door where it was installed in 1969.

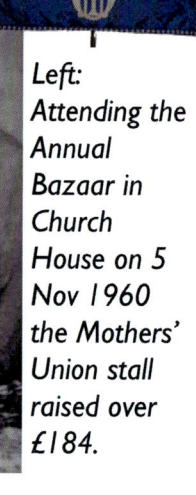

Left: Attending the Annual Bazaar in Church House on 5 Nov 1960 the Mothers' Union stall raised over £184.

The Kirkbymoorside Elderberry Club was started when the Rev. Michael Wright and Mr Jack Lynas from West Lund donated funds to start a weekly club for the over 60s. In 1976 it been a registered charity. It is still going today and is an inter-faith club and the trustees are currently Father McCabe Rev. Davey and Rev. Stephens. Members meet to socialise, play dominos and whist. There have always been outings and an annual lunch at Christmas. The group used to meet in the Church House until it was leased to NYCC in 2009. Here are a couple of photos of some of the original members in the 1970s.

# Chapter Ten: The Petch Family Of Kirkbymoorside and Their Connection With All Saints Church

In the north aisle of the church is a window, depicting the Good Shepherd, dedicated to the memory of several nineteenth century members of the Petch family. Underneath, the last local descendant of the family to bear the name installed a plaque which reads: "In affectionate memory of John Petch, the last practising member of an old legal family long connected with this church and town."

This connection between the town, the Petch family and the church began in the late eighteenth century when an earlier John Petch moved to Kirkbymoorside from Glaisdale to work as a solicitor, probably in partnership with his elder brother George.

Untangling the generations that followed is complicated by the fact that men in this branch of the Petch family had only three names between them: Robert (the eldest in each generation), George and John. Most improbably, no fewer than three successive Roberts married a Mary, and several daughters were of course given this name!

In or about 1785 the John who moved to Kirkbymoorside from Glaisdale built (or bought – the evidence is conflicting) the house on Howe End which bears the Petch name. He was already married to Ann Cook of

Danby, and they settled down to have four children (of whom only one, Robert, lived into adulthood). We know nothing of John's relationship with the church but can assume it was shaky at some point because when Ann died of dropsy aged 40 in 1797, John proceeded to marry her much younger sister. While this was legal, it was not acceptable to the Church of England, and required a special dispensation from the Archbishop of York, which may still be seen in the county archives in Northallerton. John died in 1818, but Hannah, his second wife, lived until 1836, the year after marriages such as hers were finally prohibited by law (which did not, however, invalidate those that had already taken place). It was not until 1907 that it again became legal for a man to marry his deceased wife's sister. We may assume however that John himself thought the sisters would approve of this arrangement, as the three of them are buried together beneath an impressive table tomb in All Saints churchyard.

John's eldest son and heir, Robert, is remembered in the window, along with his wife Mary (née Harrison), daughter of the town surgeon. She was described as a woman "with bewitching curls", whom he courted from the age of 16, and finally married at 27. This portrait of Mary is housed in the Scarborough Art Gallery. The window also remembers two of their six children, son Robert, and daughter Mary: why the other children were not included is not known.

Among these other children was George, the only member of the immediate family to enter the church, becoming Rector of Oddington in Otmoor (Oxfordshire), a living in the gift of Trinity College, in 1857.

In the same year, he married Ann Lesley (right), daughter of his brother Robert's wife's sister. "*My father had a clear remembrance*" his daughter Agnes recalled "*of riding over on his pony in the year 1835 from Kirby to Sinnington when he was nine years old, to inquire for Mrs Lesley and the baby. That baby was destined to be his wife and my own mother.*"

They had three other daughters in addition to Agnes: Henrietta, Katie and Gertrude.

The four daughters of George Petch were frequent visitors to the house on Howe End, where they made the acquaintance of the children of Walter Guy Ketchley, who was vicar of Kirkbymoorside from 1877 to 1905. Two of these Petch girls proceeded to marry two of the Ketchley boys, both of whom entered the church. Walter Ketchley married Katie Petch in 1883. Harry Ketchley's marriage to Henrietta Petch, which took place in 1885, seems somewhat less conventional. Henrietta, according to her sister, was the beauty of the family and somewhat temperamental.

In 1890 they moved to Romsey (Hampshire) where Harry was curate; then in 1894 he became rector of Barton le Street, near to his old home. But Henrietta was living in Chideok St Giles in Dorset (near her sister Gertrude), and their two daughters were at boarding school. She is described on the 1890 census as head of household and artist. Shortly after that, however, she returned to Barton, suffering from diabetes, and died there in 1904. She is not buried in Barton, and for a while her grave eluded us until we – almost literally – stumbled over her near the door of All Saints Kirkbymoorside. Her father in law, Walter Guy Ketchley, died a few days before she did, and there seems to have been a family funeral which saw them interred in adjacent plots. Harry married again some years later, left Barton, and lived in Pickering, apparently without employment, before becoming rector of Biddestone in Wiltshire and later canon.

Young Robert Petch (grandson of John) had six children, of whom four survived to adulthood. The eldest surviving of these was a daughter, Ann (b 1851), who, like her aunts, looked to the local clergy for a husband. She became engaged to Thomas Stephens during his brief spell as curate in Kirkbymoorside, but he was poor and they were to wait ten years for him to find a living which would support a wife. The living, when it came, was a good one, at Horsley in Northumberland, where the old vicarage is still testimony to days of more gracious living, although the village is small and isolated. They married in 1886. Ann was already 36, and died at 46; she is buried in Horsley, along with the elder of her two daughters who died aged 14; the younger seems to have stayed at home to look after her father who remained in harness until his death at the age of 81 in 1924.

John (left) was the last Petch to become a solicitor and inherit the family business in Kirkbymoorside and the house on Howe End on his father's death in 1889. He married Elizabeth Hebden, but had only one child, a daughter, Irene, born in 1899. Women were admitted as solicitors for the first time in 1922, when Irene was 23, but the notion of her entering the family profession seems not to have occurred to anyone, and so John became "the last practising member of an old legal family" commemorated in the church plaque.

Some time around 1900, the family abandoned the house on Howe End and moved to a newly built one, Howe Green, at the end of Swineherd Lane. The old house languished somewhat, rented out, until 1954 when Irene, mindful no doubt of death duties, gave it to the Church of England pensions board. They used it for a while to house the widows of clergymen, but it was probably something of a white elephant, and the Church sold it in 1968, shortly after Irene's death.

Irene was a published poet, her first anthology, "The Waiting Room" appearing in 1931. In 1935 she wrote "The Parish

THE PETCH HOUSE WAS BUILT ABOUT 1785 BY JOHN PETCH, WHO SETTLED AT KIRBYMOORSIDE; HE AND HIS DESCENDANTS PRACTISING AS SOLICITORS HERE, IN UNBROKEN SUCCESSION UNTIL THE DEATH OF THE LAST JOHN PETCH IN 1929. GIVEN IN 1954 BY HIS DAUGHTER IRENE PETCH

Church", which appeared on the back of a little guide book, laboriously titled "The Story of Kirkbymoorside with Gillamoor and Bransdale and Farndale Churches", published that same year. Otherwise Irene's poetry was largely secular and concerned with the wild beauty of the local landscape.

Irene died, unmarried, in 1965, leaving an estate of £64,594:10:0, of which some £28,000 went in estate duty. Her will contained a multiplicity of charitable bequests, including the following:

"*Our Lord greatly honoured animals by being born amongst them and His unqualified assertion that no falling sparrow is forgotten before God shatters every excuse for any mishandling of the creatures entrusted to us by their Creator and ours – 'Be ye merciful as your Father also is merciful' – and I feel that we as members of His Church should do everything in our power to help the animals which He honoured. I therefore leave to the Parochial Church Council of the Parish of Kirkbymoorside in memory of my Father and Mother the sum of one hundred pounds. It is my wish that special sermons (which if desired may be obtained from the Royal Society for the Prevention of Cruelty to Animals) on the promotion of kindness and the prevention of cruelty to animals be preached and special prayers for the same purpose used annually on the Fourth Sunday after Trinity in the Parish Church of Kirkbymoorside at Mattins and Evensong and the collections at such services given to the Royal Society for the Prevention of Cruelty to Animals.*" Was this request ever honoured?

Irene also left £100 to the Parochial Church Council of Kirkbymoorside "*to be applied in keeping the graves and headstones of my grandparents,*

*parents and myself in good order and repair*" which has certainly not been done. Although local residents recall Irene's funeral complete with black horses, and her name appears on the burial register, there is no grave number and her actual grave can no longer be located.

Petch House formerly known as Meadow Way

Dedicated to the 'practising members of an old legal family': John Petch(1757-1818), his son Robert Petch (1786-1839), his grandson Robert Petch (1815-1889), and his great grandson John Petch (1856-1929), and to his great great granddaughter Irene Petch (1899-1965). Thank you for a lovely house.

Jean Richards, The Petch House.

**The Parish Church** - *Irene Petch, April 1935*

Grey Mother Church - as Jesus long ago

Commanded little children to be brought

That he might draw them to Him and bestow

His blessing on them, so you, who have caught

The spirit of His teaching, open wide

Your arms today, and take each helpless child

And bless it in His name.

                                        Vigilant Guide,

Warning your children lest they be beguiled

By earthly things. You take them by the hand

And lead them confidently down the years,

Strengthening them so that they may withstand

The storms of life, and quietening their fears;

Rejoicing in their Spring and joining them

In holy wedlock; sharing all their deep

Sorrows and joys, alert and swift to stem

The rising tide of worldliness and to keep

Those hurtful things away which smirch the soul.

Grey Mother Church - the red roofs cluster round,

Huddle together, seeking your protection;

This green quiet garden, this most holy ground

Has held the loyalty and the affections

Of generations. Through the centuries
How many bridegrooms, and how many brides,
How many slow processions, have walked these
Smooth well-worn stones? Alas, how Time derides!
They all have vanished; and there now survives
No shadow of their wisdom or their skill,
No trace of their laborious honest lives,
And yet about this place there lingers still
The spirit of the past, a mellow peace,
And with the ancient quietude are blent
Small country sounds: a little rustling breeze,
A sparrow's homely chirrup of content,
A lamb's thin cry, the mother's answering bleat,
The haunting sweetness of a blackbird's song.
Here life and death foregather, here they meet
Among the lichened tombstones-death so strong,
So palpably victorious…Yet that tree,
Which through the winter looked so bare and dead,
Now challenges death's seeming victory
For each pale downy Chestnut bud had shed
Its varnished scales, has burst its prisoning sheath.
So, one day, shall these sleeping bodies fling
Away their bonds, shall break the seals of death,
And awaken to an everlasting Spring.

# Chapter Eleven: Extracts from Twenty Years (1919 – 1939) of The Kirkby Moorside Parish Magazine

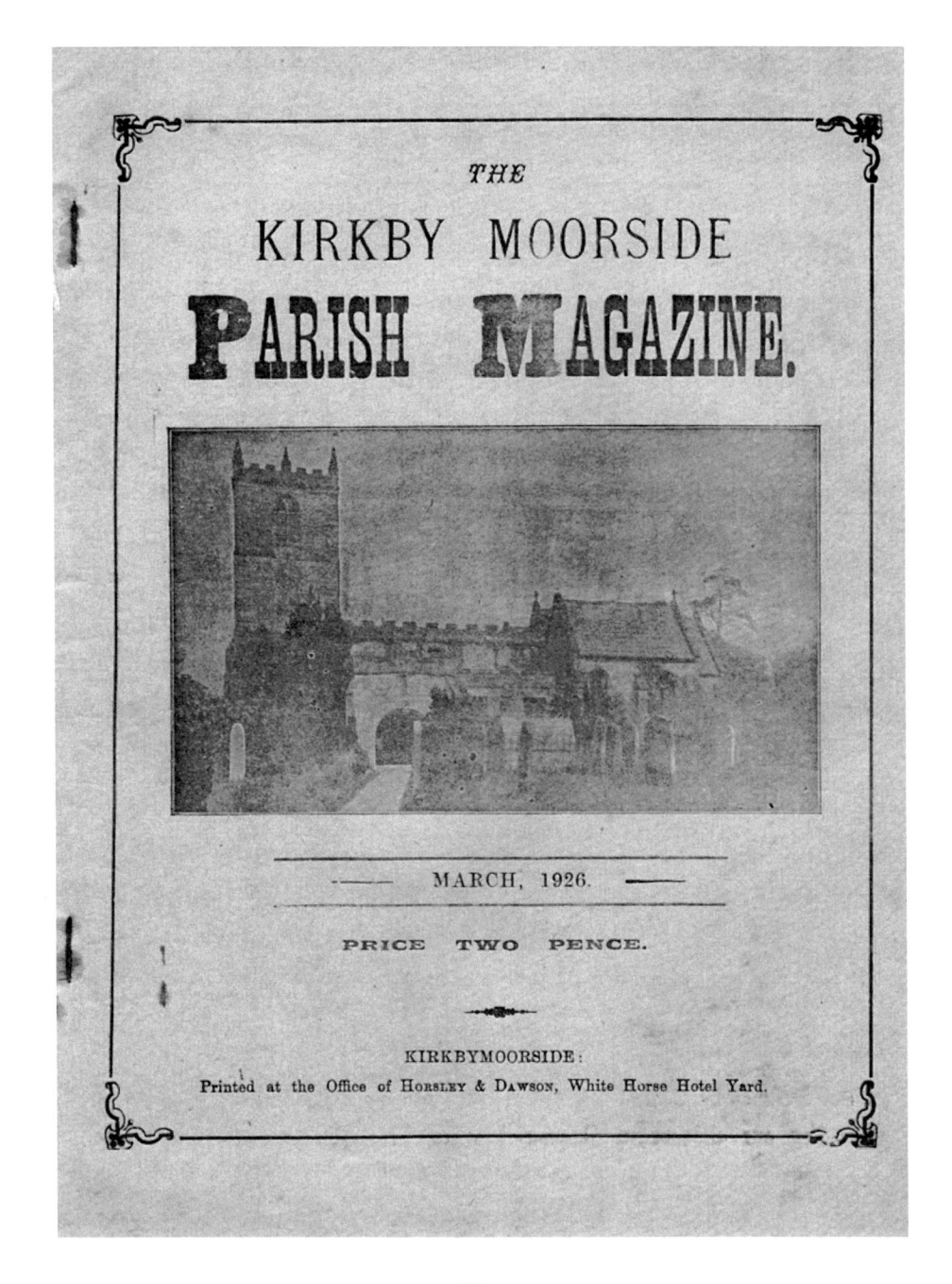

## THE KIRKBY MOORSIDE PARISH MAGAZINE.

MARCH, 1926.

PRICE TWO PENCE.

KIRKBYMOORSIDE:
Printed at the Office of Horsley & Dawson, White Horse Hotel Yard.

# Church of All Saints', Kirkbymoorside.

*Clergy*: A. S. HARNBY, B.A., Hon. C.F. (Vicar), Surrogate.
*Churchwardens*: Mr. C. E. BODDY, Vicar's Warden.
   Mr. KNEESHAW WALKER, People's Warden.
*Organist*: Mr. G. F. FLETCHER, A.R.C.M., L.R.A.M.
*Church Council* 1926: Messrs. J. Anderson, J. BAXTER, C. E. BODDY, J. H. DOBSON, G. DONKIN, J. BOWES, W. P. FRANK, J. C. FRANK, G. F. FLETCHER, Capt. C. SCOTT-HOPKINS, Messrs. T. ISHERWOOD, J. PETCH, F. RICKABY, J. RICKABY, G. SIMPSON, J. STURDY, T. TAYLOR, K. WALKER, A. PEACE. Mesdames BURNETT, COOPER, HILL, HARNBY, A. JACKSON, C. RICKABY, C. WALKER. Misses I. PETCH, E. WOOD, L. WOOD.

## Services.

HOLY COMMUNION Sundays and Holy Days.
   1st Sunday in the month—Holy Communion 8 a.m & 11.15 a.m.
MATINS: Sundays at 10.30 a.m.
EVENSONG: Sundays at 6.30 p.m.
CHILDREN'S SERVICE: On the third Sunday in the month, at 9-30 a.m
   Sunday School at 2. p.m.
HOLY BAPTISMS by arrangement. Churchings before any of the Services.
MARRIAGES between 8 a.m. and 3 p.m. Notice of Banns to be given personally to the Vicar. The Fees (inclusive) are Banns 6/6, Licence 15/-. A Licence costs 40/- (in addition) and may be obtained from the Vicar.
The Vicar is ready at all hours to visit the sick. Immediate notice should be sent.
   The Church is open all day for private prayer and meditation.
Daily Matins at 8 a.m. Daily Evensong at 5-30 p.m. (Except otherwise stated).

## Gillamoor.

*Churchwardens*: Messrs. G. SIMPSON and J. AINSLEY.
*Organist*: Mr. J. BAXTER.   *Clerk*: Mr. C. LENG.

## Services.

HOLY COMMUNION once a month. See Calendar for day and time.
SUNDAYS: Evensong and Sermon at 2.30 p.m

## 1919

- 18 September Bishop Beverley dedicated the carved oak chancel screen with gifts. This was a gift from Mr and Mrs Holt, designed by Temple Moore and the work being executed by Thompson's of Peterborough with the following inscription:
" *To The Honour and Glory of God and in grateful memory of those who fought and died for their country in The Great War 1914 – 1918.*"

*Printed in the office of Mr Coultman, Chemist and Stationer*

## 1921

- John Harker died Wed. 9 March aged 81yrs old. He was Postmaster in Kirby for 30 years and was also the founder of Harker's String Band which was well known in Ryedale.

*Printed in the office of Horsley and Dawson, White Horse Hotel Yard.*

## 1923

- 600 eggs were sent from the The Children's Service to two Leeds Hospitals
- 11 December Rev. Brown from York gave a Lantern Lecture in the Church House on Japan. A collection was made for SPG Earthquake Fund following the disastrous Japanese earthquake.

## 1924

- August – Kirkbymoorside Choir and Bell Ringers went on a trip to Wembley which was "*enjoyed as never a trip was enjoyed.*" Local M.P. Sir Charles Wilson escorted them round the House of Commons and the Chapel. At Wembley the group met up with the former vicar Rev. Willson for tea.
- 5 July – the death of Robert Walker of Dale End House at the age of 90 yrs was the last entry to be made in a Burial Register opened by the late Rev. W G Ketchley on 18 December 1880. The third entry of the register records the burial of the widow of Rev. Edmund Gray who became Vicar of Kirby in April 1826. "*It is a link with nearly 100 years of parish history.*"

# ADVERTISEMENTS.

## JOHN BURNETT,
Pharmaceutical Chemist,
WINE AND SPIRIT MERCHANT.

PURE DRUGS & CHEMICALS.

Photographic Requisites

GENUINE WINES AND SPIRITS

TONTINE HOUSE,

KIRBYMOORSIDE.

**C**an
**O**ffer
**U**seful
**L**ines
**T**ogether with
**M**any
**A**ttractive
**N**ew
**S**pecialities for 1926.

Chemist & Stationer,
Kirbymoorside.

## Ernest Sherwood,
Ladies' and Gent's TAILOR
and General Outfitter,

Howe End, KIRBYMOORSIDE.

Ready Made Clothing
of every description.

## ROBT. E. WATSON,
**Railway Street, Kirbymoorside**

Groceries and Provisions of the Highest Quality
:-:   :-:   at Lowest Market Prices.   :-:   :-.

Finest Breakfast Bacon.   All Best Brands of Tinned Goods, Jams, etc.
For a Delicious Cup of Tea Always Use our Special Blend.
Try our Celebrated Baking Powder 10d. per 1b.

**1925**

- For the Confirmation on 2 June the Archbishop was present. Confirmation classes were to be held in the Church House on Mondays at 7.15pm.
- Mr Arthur Wood celebrated 50 yrs as a bell ringer. He first rang the bells on the anniversary of Queen Victoria's birthday 24 May 1875.
- Royal visit in July by Princess Mary to open the Yorkshire Children's Hospital – also the vicar quoted these details of a previous royal celebration. When the Queen Mother married in 1863, Kirkbymoorside organised the following:

*"I. 12 noon Old Men and Labourers shall be entertained at the Toll Booth with beef, bread and ale*
*II. 3pm Old Women and Labourers' Wives shall be entertained at the Toll Booth with tea and cakes.*
*III. 7 pm There shall be a display of fireworks in the Market Place and a bonfire lighted on the Volunteer drill-ground, above the Church.*
*All persons joining the procession should provide themselves with a white favour to be worn on the left breast."*

- Church House news – Wireless Club is now open to members. Apply to Miss L Wood
- Sunday School prizes were awarded. 110 books were awarded, that being the number of children on the register. Full marks were gained by Jerry Sleightholme, Ernest Rivis, Eileen Sleightholme and Cynthia & Frances Farrow

**1926**

- The War Memorial Tablet which listed those enrolled as well as those who fell in the Great War was dedicated on 25 Dec 1925. This was a gift of the late Vicar, Rev. H E Willson and Mrs Willson.
- New Year Message:

*"Here is a reminder that another milestone is passed on the Great High Road to Eternity, and that our Pilgrimage is one restless marching until God calls a halt.*

## Everything connected with the family table
### CAN BE HAD AT
# A. E. SONLEY'S,
#### High Class Food Distributor,
#### Market Place and West End, Kirbymoorside.

All the leading brands of Bacon, Tea, Coffee etc.

Home-made Bread and Cakes a speciality.

Our Vans maintain a regular service throughout Ryedale.

---

## For Best Value in Fruit, Flowers, Vegetables and Sweets—Shop at
# F. & K. LEEK,
### Fruiterers & Confectioners
## MARKET PLACE, KIRBYMOORSIDE.
*"Where the Buses Stop."*

---

# W. R. NICHOL
(successor to the late H. Clare Senior)
Telephone 35.

### STATIONERY

BASILDON BOND,
ROYAL & ANCIENT
and all Fancy Stationery.

Waterman and Swan Pens.
Business Envelopes.
Account Books, &c.
**Lending Library.**

For PURE DRUGS,
PROMPT ATTENTION
PROVED SPECIALITIES
SHOP AT
**W. R. NICHOL.**

Special attention paid to dispensing of doctor's prescriptions and family recipes.

Agent for Thorleys Foods, &c.
Carter's Seeds (all kinds),
and all the well known Sheep Dips,
and Cattle Medicines.

> *A sacred burden is the life ye bear*
> *Look on it, lift it, bear it solemnly;*
> *Stand up and walk beneath it steadfastly*
> *Fail not for sorrow, falter not for sin*
> *But onward, upward, till ye goal ye win."*

- Rules for admission to the Girls' Friendly Society were as follows:

1. Members shall be girls and young women from the age of 12 upwards
2. Girls are not admitted contrary to the wishes of their parents
3. Members need not necessarily belong to the Church of England

The object of the society was "*to unite for the glory of God, in one Fellowship of Prayer and Service, the Girls and Women of the Empire, to uphold purity of Thought, Word and Deed.*"

## 1928

- Girls Friendly Society had its opening meeting on 6 November. The baptism Roll was started where babies names were placed on this list and their birthdays would be noted by receipt of a card. This was to keep in even closer touch with prospective Sunday School scholars. "Sunday School must be made to mean more both to parent and scholar…if our children are to be rooted and grounded in the Faith."

## 1929

- A box with 500 eggs was sent to the Women & Children's Hospital in Leeds, from the Egg Service and another gift sent to the Yorkshire Children's Orthopaedic Hospital.
- Mr John Petch, the last practising member of a prominent family of lawyers was buried on 2 April, "*when a very large and representative congregation*" gathered to pay their respects.
- 'A truly great Ryedale character' described Mrs Harriet Baker, who was laid to rest on 12 April. "*She has been known to us…as one of the keenest business women in the district, and as one who held an unchallenged position as the head of a large family which regarded her with the utmost respect.*"

## WALKERS
### for
### Boots and Shoes.
Established 1777.

Repairs a Speciality.

**Crown Square,
Kirbymoorside.**

---

## Dennis Hill & Son
### Watchmakers & Jewellers.

FISHING TACKLE.

**MARKET PLACE,
KIRBYMOORSIDE.**

---

## J. W. Helm & Son
### High-Class Grocers and Provision Merchants

Pure Coffee ground as required. Best quality Bacon and delicious Butter and Cheese.

**MARKET PLACE,
KIRBYMOORSIDE.**

---

## Frank Hammond
### Florist,
### Fruiterer & Seedsman,

Wreaths and Bouquets.

**West End, Kirbymoorside**

---

## SCARBOROUGH HOSPITAL CONTRIBUTORY SCHEME.

On the Register of **Kirbymoorside Branch** there are **620** names.

*Is YOUR Name on any Register of this Scheme?*

Insure against possible Hospital Expenses.

Mrs. E. HILL, Market Place, Hon. Sec.
Mr. W. H. F. HOODLESS, Midland Bank, Hon. Treas.

---

## PICKERING & DISTRICT CO-OPERATIVE SOC'Y LTD.

Central Premises & Reg'd Office: Southgate, Pickering
Branches: Kirbymoorside, Helmsley & Thornton Dale.

### Dealers in
### High-Class Groceries, Provisions, Drapery,
### Boots & Shoes, etc.

SATISFACTION GUARANTEED.
FREE LIFE ASSURANCE (Husband & Wife).
PROFITS SHARED AMONG MEMBERS.

Members and others in Kirbymoorside District are invited to visit our New Branch Premises, which we claim to be the finest Shop in the District.

**Shop at the Co-op.**

**1933**
- The impressive record of service on the part of the choir men received wide publicity in the press:
    Mr J Sturdy 60 yrs
    Mr A Wood 54 yrs
    Mr John Rickaby 50 yrs
    Mr John Anderson 50 yrs
    Mr Hartley Rutter 50 yrs

**1934 April** – Rev Harnby took the opportunity to voice his feelings on people leaving litter about – "*These are those who have no eye for beauty whatever, who by their careless acts leave eyesores wherever they go. And they are not only children, although the latter badly need to learn ... what not to do with their litter. Workmen who dig up our roads.. ought to clear all their litter away. We have all seen old, rusted pipes lying about the roadside for months. Who is responsible?.....A supper may be all the tastier when eaten from a flat tombstone but why leave the 'plate' behind for someone to remove the next morning?*"

Continuing on he also queried the spirit of restlessness at weekends; hikers, cyclists and motorists were all asked "*what value is placed on Sunday, either as a day of rest, or as a day of worship, by these moving multitudes. Has worship lost its appeal to many? Is it out of date?....There is much at is wrong and selfish here ... neglect of worship impoverishes the individual character and ... a world not keen on worship can never raise itself out of the rut in which it is now stuck.*"

**1936**
- Rev Harnby welcomed back Mr John W Bowes, who retired from service with the LNER Company in December after 45yrs, ending his career as Station Master at Birstwith Harrogate. He was described as an enthusiastic chorister "*in love with All Saints' Choir as much as any*" it was hoped he would become a regular once more.

**1937**
- Annual Meeting of the Nursing Association met at Church House. Mrs Harrison Holt presided where she spoke of the great

# HOME-MADE BREAD, CAKES AND PASTRIES

supplied by

## SAMPLES,

The Market Place,

Kirbymoorside.

※ ※

**Refreshments and Teas.**

---

# DAWSON.

Wet and Fried

## FISH

Daily.

Supper = Room.

Crown Square,
Kirbymoorside.

---

# G. Cooper & Sons
(Pickering) Ltd.

Furnishing and
General Ironmongers,

**Glass and China Merchants**

Sporting Cartridges,
Cream Separators,
Cutlery, etc
Stockists of ALADDIN LAMPS

**MARKET PLACE,**
KIRBYMOORSIDE.
TEL. 222.

---

# HARRY KING,

Cabinet Maker

and

Undertaker.

Upholsterer & Antique Furniture Dealer.

West End, Kirbymoorside

loss in the death of Sir Gervase Beckett. The annual report stated that over 3050 visits were paid by nurses during the year.
- The Scarborough Hospital Contributory Scheme was well supported by the town with 120 paying into the fund. £5,900 had been raised that year by contributions. *"Our patients who go into hospital are now under this scheme so relieving them of financial worry."*
- May saw the Coronation of King George VI and Elizabeth.
- A jumble sale for the Waifs and Strays Society raised £16/7s/1d.

## 1938

- Mrs McCormick's new revue "Hurdy Gurdy" was said to be the best yet produced. It was to be staged in the Memorial Hall on Tuesday 17 January for the benefit of Church funds
- A whist drive was held at Fadmoor and with a dance to follow with music provided by Timothy's Accordion Dance Band. Entrance fee was 1/- with refreshments at reasonable charges.
- Mr John Craven Frank, the manager of Barclay's Bank retired.
- Rudland School closed on 31 October. It was built by the Earl of Feversham and opened on 25 September 1905 and for 33 years taught children from the surrounding area. Mrs Mowforth was the teacher and the old school was to become a Chapel.
- December – The issue of The Jewish & Christian Refugees. The Church Of England pledged £50,000 to the resettlement of persecuted Christian Jews from Germany.

## 1939

- May – *"We congratulate Mr Harry Rickaby on his recent appointment as Headmaster of Council School at Leeming, Northallerton. It is very pleasing to note this success of one of our old boys, and we hope that this is but the first of further rises in his profession."*
- Mr J W Hill of Castlegate died 11 May, aged 67 yrs. He was a well-known figure who served the Church as Churchwarden and sidesman. He had also been involved in the Air-Raid Precaution Work.

## Marmaduke Place

Painter, Paperhanger, etc.

A SPLENDID SELECTION OF WALL PAPERS ALWAYS IN STOCK.

PIERCY END and HOWE END,
**KIRBYMOORSIDE.**

## Horsley & Dawson

(Proprietor: A. H. Watson)

General Printers, Bookbinders and Stationers.

Howe End, Kirbymoorside.

---

The CHURCH HOUSE, Kirbymoorside, is available for all kinds of PUBLIC and COMMITTEE MEETINGS.

Apply: Mr. G. RICHARDSON.

---

## ERNEST SHERWOOD

Ladies' & Gent's Tailor,
*Complete Outfitter.*
*Breeches Specialist.*

Mourning Orders promptly executed.

Agent for Emcodine Waterproof Garments.

*Howe End, Kirbymoorside.*

## The Manchester Unity of Oddfellows,

AGRICULTURAL LODGE, KIRBYMOORSIDE,

IS THE

Friendly Society for You.

All particulars from
**Mr. T. BOWES,**
Carlton House, Kirbymoorside.

---

## C. ARTHUR BODDY AND SONS,

Corn Millers and Factors, Dealer in Cake, Seeds, &c.,

**Roller Flour Mill, Kirby Mills, Kirbymoorside.**
Also VIVER'S MILL, PICKERING

Entwistle's Poultry Foods — Grinding in all its branches.

CHARGES FOR GRINDING :—Pig Corn 1d. per stone, 1½d. if carted. Wheat for Flour 4/- per sack, anything less 3d. per stone. Anywhere where our wagons go will be carted free of charge.

- The Loyal Agricultural Lodge of Kirbymoorside which was a lodge of the Manchester Unity Friendly Society made history by celebrating 100yrs. A centenary dinner was held in the Memorial Hall on Thursday 18 May with a large gathering of members and friends. The Grandmaster Brother F Cundall and the secretary was Mr Tom Bowes. The movement began with seven members who met at the Red Lion Inn.

This is the story of All Saints to date.

The church at the head of the moors has continued to thrive thanks to the efforts and dedication of not just the clergy but of the ordinary townsfolk. Without those willing to polish the brass and woodwork, chase cobwebs and dust from the stalls and windows and cut the grass, the church would soon fall into a state of neglect. Contributions of gifts from local craftsmen, such as Wilf Dowson and the patronage of the local gentry have left a legacy for future generations to build upon.

This work is dedicated to all those who have gone before and are still to come.